# BEANS, GRAINS, NUTS & SEEDS

### FURTHER ADVENTURES IN EATING CLOSE TO HOME

# FURTHER ADVENTURES

# BEANS, GRAINS, NUTS & SEEDS

## IN EATING CLOSE TO HOME

ELIN KRISTINA ENGLAND

Elin would love to know about
your further adventures in eating close to home.
You can reach her at elin.england@gmail.com

Beans, Grains, Nuts & Seeds: Further Adventures
in Eating Close to Home / November 2013
All rights reserved.
Copyright © 2013 by Elin Kristina England.
Author photo by Kory Schneider.
Front cover by Gray Design.
Page design by Gray Design and Lynn Marx.
Production and copy editing by Lynn Marx.

ISBN 978-0-578-13364-5

THIS BOOK IS DEDICATED

to family farmers and gardeners worldwide

—those stalwart individuals who

patiently and doggedly steward the land,

save the seeds, and

preserve the knowledge of

how to feed us all, season after season.

On your aching backs,

cranky knees, and sunburnt necks

rests the future of humanity.

Thank you.

# GIVE THANKS

There are a great many people to whom credit should be given for assisting in the conception, gestation, development, and birthing of this book. Family, friends, co-workers — pretty much anyone who is a part of my life at this point will have heard me repeat ad nauseam "I'm working on a new book… still working on that book… the book is coming along… just about done with that book…" Thank you, all of you, for having the forbearance not to throw your collective arms in the air, cast your eyes to the heavens, mutter "yeah, right, sure, OK," and walk away as quickly as etiquette will allow.

Thanks also to the many people who served, knowingly or otherwise, as guinea pigs as I worked my way through recipe testing. Maybe you didn't see me watching you at that potluck, but your return for a second helping was duly noted.

There are a few individuals who deserve special recognition.

Marcia Rae, lately of Brownsville, and Lynne Fessenden of Willamette Farm and Food Coalition, who were really quite insistent that a book on grains and beans was needed and moreover that I should write it.

Willow Coberly and Mary Ann Jasper of Stalford Farms for that initial meeting in Brownsville during which the seed of this book was sown.

Andrew Still and Sarah Kleeger of Open Oak Farm, Kasey White and Jeff Broadie of Lonesome Whistle Farm, and Tom and Sue Hunton of Camas Country Mill for cheering me on from the fields and serving as my primary sources for beans and grains in this end of the valley.

Karen Guillemin, who loves playing with food as much as I do, and who provided me with many insights into the wild and wonderful world of microorganisms.

Lynn Marx, whose mastery of the intricacies of the English language and seemingly unlimited patience for detail are staggering.

Thanks to my mother and my grandmothers and to their mothers and grandmothers and to the long line of women reaching back to time immemorial who have found endless ways to combine the ingredients they had at hand, cook them up into something tasty and nourishing, and call it good.

To my incredible children, Kyra and Kory. This knowledge is your inheritance. You and your generation are my inspiration. You are miracles and gifts, both of you.

And to my husband, Don, without whose love, support, and unwavering confidence in my ability to pull this off, none of this would be possible.

# CONTENTS

**WHY BEANS, GRAINS, NUTS & SEEDS?** | 11

**BEANS, GRAINS, NUTS & SEEDS IN THE PACIFIC NORTHWEST** | 19

**BEANS** | 23
    Sprouting Beans | 28
    Bean Cooking Basics | 29

BEAN APPETIZERS
    Arikara Bean Pâté with Toasted Spices | 34
    Ceci Fritta (Fried Garbanzo Beans) | 36
    Mediterranean Lentil Tapenade | 37
    Farinata | 38
    Ireland Creek Annie Bean Bruschetta | 40
    *Red Pepper Sauce* | 41
    Winter White Bean Dip with Turnips, Lemon & Sage | 42

JUST A BOWL OF BEANS, PLEASE
    *Lemon-Walnut Cilantro Sauce* | 44
    Daniel's Black Beans | 45
    Beans with Pesto and Pistou | 46
    Braised Rosso di Lucca Beans with Rosemary and Thyme | 48
    Calypso Beans with Coconut Milk, Ginger & Black Mustard Seeds | 50
    Nabiha's Father's Way with Lentils (Chanay Ki Daal) | 52
    *Slow-Roasted Tomatoes* | 54
    *Spanish Sofrito Sauce* | 55

**BEANS AND MORE**

　Arikara Beans with Tomatillo Pork | 57
　*Pickled Onions* | 58
　*Crunchy Cabbage, Carrot & Radish Slaw* | 59
　Cannellini Beans with Fresh Grilled Tuna | 60
　Roasted Garbanzos with Garlic and Greens | 62
　Cranberry Beans Simmered with Sage, Sausages & Tomatoes | 64
　Joanna's Chili | 66
　Mediterranean-Style Pasta and Beans | 68
　Black Bean, Chorizo & Rice Stew | 70
　*Cilantro and Toasted Pumpkin Seed Sauce* | 72

**BAKED BEANS**

　Eunice's Yellow-Eyed Baked Beans | 74
　Chocolate Baked Rio Zape Beans | 76
　Farmor's Bruna Bönar (Swedish Baked Beans) | 78

**PATTIES, BURGERS & OTHER TASTY CAKES**

　*Parsley Pesto* | 79
　Cranberry Beans & Rye Patties with Sage & Walnuts | 80
　Homemade Falafel | 82
　*Lemon-Garlic Tahini Sauce* | 83
　*Tzatziki* | 83
　Bean Burgers with Greens 'n Grains | 84
　Black Bean Patties | 86
　*Quick Tomatillo Salsa (Salsa Verde)* | 87

**BEAN SALADS**

　Basic Bean Salad | 89
　Bean Salad with Wheat Berries and Quinoa | 90
　Garbanzo Bean Salad with Summer Herbs | 92
　Spring Bean Salad | 93

BEAN SOUPS AND STEWS

*Raita* | 94

Curried Lentil Soup | 95

Late Summer Lentil Stew with Roasted Vegetables | 96

Indian Woman Yellow Bean Soup with Hardy Greens | 98

North African-Style Garbanzo Bean Stew | 100

Ribollita | 102

Lemony Garbanzo Bean Soup | 104

**GRAINS** | 105

Basic Big Berry Grain Cooking | 111

Sprouting Grains | 117

GRAINS FOR BREAKFAST

Oatmeal | 119

Crockpot Grain Party Porridge | 121

Toasted Bulgur Wheat Porridge with Apples | 122

Teff, Flax & Oatmeal Porridge | 123

Basic Whole Grain Pancakes | 124

Chia Seed and Buckwheat Pancakes | 125

Teff and Ricotta Pancakes with Apple Topping | 126

Overnight Oatmeal-Sesame Pancakes | 128

Cornmeal Pancakes | 129

MAINS WITH GRAINS

Basic Polenta | 131

Polenta Pasticciata di Mama Elin | 132

Savory Teffolenta | 134

Barley Mushroom Terrine | 136

Buckwheat Crêpes | 138

*Crab and Kale Crêpe Filling* | 140

*Pear, Prune & Armagnac Crêpe Filling* | 141

Wheat Berries Arrabiata with Poached Eggs | 142
Salmon and Barley Cakes | 144
*Mushroom Cream Garnish | 146*
*Lemon-Dill Yoghurt Sauce | 146*

GRAINS ON THE SIDE... OR ON THE INSIDE!
Golden Barley Risotto with Wild Mushrooms | 148
Italian Suppli | 150
Wheat Berry Pilaf | 151
Wild Rice with Cranberries and Caramelized Onions | 152

GRAIN SALADS
Purple Barley Salad with Apple and Celery | 154
Roast Roots 'n Rye | 156
Wheat Berry Salad with Broccoli, Apple, Hazelnuts & Smoked Salmon | 158
Summer Grain Salad | 160

GRAIN SOUPS AND STEWS
Barley Beef Stew with Mushrooms | 162
Bulgur Wheat Soup with Lentils and Winter Greens | 164
Frikeh and Buttermilk Soup | 166
Minestrone with Wheat Berries and Arugula Pesto | 168
Smoky Tomato Soup with Quinoa | 170
Winter Squash Stew with Purple Barley | 172

**EASY BAKED GOODS**

Corn Crisps | *175*

Corn Pones | *176*

Spoonbread | *177*

Spicy Nutty Apple Rye Muffins | *178*

Overnight Oatcakes | *180*

Chef Zachary's Unbelievable Buttermilk Biscuits | *182*

**GRAINS FOR DESSERT**

A Simple Fruit Crumble | *183*

Dolce di Grano | *184*

Spelt-Hazelnut Cookies | *185*

Teff Chocolate Chip Cookies—Two ways | *186*

Not Your Nonna's Biscotti | *188*

Golden Hulless Barley Pudding with Fruit Compote | *190*

Indian Pudding | *192*

**FURTHER ADVENTURES WITH GRAINS**

Nixtamal | *194*

Hominy | *195*

Hominy with Chile and Tomato Braised Meat | *196*

Homemade Tortillas | *198*

*Basic Salsa* | *199*

Jennifer's Sort-of Posole | *200*

Posole Soup with Beans | *201*

Farmor's Limpa | *202*

Sourdough Rye Starter | *204*

Sourdough Rye Bread | *206*

**NUTS AND SEEDS** | *207*

    Harvesting Nuts | *209*

    Cooking with Nuts and Seeds | *210*

    Sprouting Nuts | *211*

**NUTS & SEEDS IN BAKED GOODS & DESSERTS**

    Dried Fruit and Nut Crostini | *212*

    Hazelnut Crackers | *214*

    Farmor's Hazelnut Cookies | *216*

    Claudia's Hazelnut Cookies | *217*

    Panforte | *218*

    Sugar Plums | *220*

**NUTTY NIBBLES AND SEEDY BARS**

    Spicy Rosemary Hazelnuts with Orange Zest | *221*

    Elkdream Bars | *222*

    Fruit and Nut Energy Bars | *224*

**SEEDY (AND NUTTY) SPREADS, SAUCES & SEASONINGS**

    Walnut-Olive Spread | *225*

    Hazelnut Hummus | *226*

    Elin's Basil Pesto | *227*

    Romesco Sauce | *228*

    Dukkah | *230*

    Sort-of Furikake | *231*

**A FEW FINAL THOUGHTS** | *233*

**CONTRIBUTORS** | *234*

**REFERENCES AND RESOURCES** | *237*

**INDEX** | *240*

There are things you do because
they feel right and they may make no sense
and they make no money,
and it may be the real reason we are here:
to love each other and eat each other's cooking
and say that it was good.

— Brian Andreas, "Real Reason"

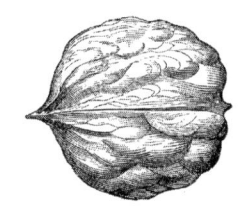

# WHY BEANS, GRAINS, NUTS & SEEDS?

Can we feed ourselves? It's a question being asked with increasing frequency. And happily, the answer appears to be yes. The proliferation of farmers markets and CSA programs across the country makes it easy to purchase locally grown fruits and vegetables. Local cheesemakers and brewers are offering award-winning regional fare. Thanksgiving turkeys and wonderful roasting chickens raised in nearby pastures are increasingly available, and grass-fed local beef, pork, and lamb are also easy to find. The fruits of the ocean are harvested by local fisherfolk and brought inland for our delectation.

So what's missing? Well, think about what you eat on a regular basis, probably several times a day. Cereal for breakfast, a sandwich for lunch, rice with dinner, pie for dessert. Refined or whole, gluten-free or not, we eat a lot of grain! Beans, too, are a common staple, albeit usually from a can, and nut butter of one sort or another is found in most kitchens across the U.S.

Beans, grains, nuts, and seeds. Together, these foods form the fourth cornerstone—a crucial component in the foundation of a vibrant, local food system.

Most people have no problem finding ways to bring more local dairy products and animal proteins into their diet. And ideas for cooking with the abundance of fruits and vegetables we grow in the Pacific Northwest pop up regularly in cooking magazines, food blogs, and cookbooks. But integrating whole grains and dry beans into our regular cooking routines can be a bit more challenging. What do you do with a sack of wheat berries? How do you cook those beautiful dried beans you just picked up at the farmers market? What is to be done with a bag of hazelnuts or walnuts in the shell?

A few years ago, as the Willamette Valley Bean and Grain Project was really getting going, a few people approached me with the idea of writing a book about cooking with all of the beans and grains that were being reintroduced to the Pacific Northwest. Knowing that wheat and dry beans can be grown in this region is great, but farmers need people to buy the stuff! And so the idea for this book was born. Despite being a fairly adventurous cook, like most people, I tended to rely more on canned beans for my day-to-day cooking, used oats mostly for breakfast, and aside from putting barley in my soup, I was a bit at a loss for what to do with it.

So I set about researching and cooking, and in the process, I've grown quite passionate about whole grains and beans. Consider the list of beans currently found in my pantry: Brightstone, garbanzo, Tigers Eye, Rossa di Lucca, Arikara, King of the Early, Calypso, Rio Zape, Dutch Bullet, Cherokee Trail of Tears, Indian Woman Yellow, Vermont Cranberry, Swedish Brown, Turkey Craw, and several different varieties of lentils. I have, in buckets under the stairs, two types of wheat berries, a quantity of rye berries, hulless barley, naked oats, and whole corn ready to be ground into polenta. Boxes of hazelnuts and a bag of walnuts vie for space with shoes in the front hall. Reading the list of dry beans in seed catalogues leaves me a bit breathless and weak in the knees. In short, I'm hooked.

At the same time that I was starting to work out what to do with all these lovely beans and grains, others were starting to take an interest in them, too. Following the "what's old is new again" state of mind, great chefs across the country are singing the praises of heirloom beans and waxing lyrical about the subtle, grassy overtones of certain varieties of wheat. One might even say that beans and grains are "trending."

**ABOUT THIS BOOK AND HOW I COOK**

This book is meant to whet your appetite for beans, grains, nuts, and seeds. It is an introduction and an invitation to explore further. It is by no means comprehensive. There are hundreds of varieties of beans and grains, and cooking techniques for both to be found in countries all over the world. If they were collected into one book, you would need a forklift to pick it up! I am rooted amongst the tall firs and big leaf maples of the northwest coast of North America. The seasons, the soil, and the particular vagaries of weather that we are accustomed to working with here have informed my diet and my cooking style. So, the majority of the recipes I offer utilize beans, grains, nuts, and seeds that can be procured from local farmers. If you are reading this book in a location outside of the damp and mossy Pacific Northwest, you will have a host of different beans and grains at your disposal. Lucky you! Take these recipes as inspiration and a springboard, and come up with your own collection!

In a perfect world, I would be found happily buzzing about the kitchen making cheese and yoghurt, canning vegetables, baking bread from scratch, and churning out regular batches of homemade granola, crackers, pizza, and other such delights to feed my family, the members of which would all willingly participate in the planting, harvesting, cooking, and clean-up of all the above efforts. Sadly, the reality is that I have a full-time job outside the home, a very large kitchen garden and an even larger orchard to tend, a family to care for (all of whom have similarly busy lives and are not overly inclined to offer their services in the kitchen on a daily basis), and an irritating need for regular and substantial amounts of sleep.

Consequently, the perfect world very rarely becomes reality for me, or at least not for sustained periods of time. It may be that the same is true for you. I wrote this book for the majority of people in America who, at this point in time, are leading extremely busy lives. Workplace demands, childcare demands, eldercare demands, and other societal pressures all contribute to the sense — no, the reality, that there is precious little time remaining for the production of elaborate meals. Most of the recipes in this book are simple, come together fairly quickly, or can be completed piecemeal in small chunks of time. For the most part, the recipes do not require the purchase of exotic or expensive ingredients, and all are open to variation according to what you have on hand or what your personal tastes are. Most can be adjusted to fit various dietary restrictions.

Many of the recipes, particularly those in the bean section, are vegetarian or vegan, for the simple reason that beans, when combined with grains, provide a complete protein. I do enjoy meat, but find that I feel better when I consume it in smaller quantities and less often than I once did. I use it more as a seasoning or a side dish than as a major component in a meal. I also like to know where the animal was raised, and how, and by whom, for the benefit of my health and that of the planet.

Professional and amateur chefs employ a wide range of cooking styles, from aficionados of haute cuisine, who spare no expense or expenditure of energy in the pursuit of the finest of culinary experiences, to pure food enthusiasts, for whom the focus of food preparation is about preserving and enhancing the medicinal or nutritive qualities of the ingredients rather than about presentation, mouth feel, and flavor.

My cooking style falls somewhat in the middle. I pay a lot of attention to the nutrients in the foods I eat and how to get the most out of them, but I also like to keep in mind flavor, texture, and presentation. Cost is also an important factor for me, in terms of my time, labor, and wallet, as well as the earth's economy. I favor simple dishes with just a few main ingredients. However, I like to use the freshest ingredients possible, as they have enough flavor to stand on their own with a minimum of fuss. And I love improvising in the kitchen. I enjoy the challenge of combining various bits and pieces of leftovers into a new meal as much as or more than focusing on a single recipe that I have made before. I substitute ingredients freely, playing with different vegetables, fruits, spices, herbs, nuts, and cheeses.

Measurements are another area where I often employ a good deal of leeway, other than in recipes for baked goods, where a specific amount of leavening, for instance, is necessary to achieve the desired result. When a recipe calls for onions to be sautéed in three tablespoons of olive oil, I confess that I rarely measure the oil. I simply swirl enough to coat most of the bottom of the pan—a good glug or two—and proceed from there. If you are cooking in a non-stick pan, feel free to use less. If you find that your vegetables are sticking to the skillet, add a bit more oil. The same would be true for seasonings. There is an Italian phrase that I find to be particularly relevant in my cooking: *quanto basta*, or "whatever is enough." Is a dish not spicy enough? Add more pepper. Needs more salt? Fine, add a bit more! Don't particularly care for cilantro? Leave it out, or use parsley instead.

I would like to suggest that perhaps there is no "right" way to cook. Sure, there are ways to combine certain ingredients that will increase your chances of coming up with a lofty loaf of bread rather than a hard brick, but that is more about chemistry than "rightness." Life is too short and too complex to get caught up in trying to do it right!

Although I have been found more than once standing in fascination in front of the wall of kitchen gadgets at our local kitchen shop, and although there are generally several new cookbooks on my wish list, for me cooking is not about the acquisition of the newest appliance or best knife or keeping up with the latest culinary trends. Rather, cooking is a celebration of the ingredients, the land from which they were harvested, and the individuals who nourished them. Cooking is a way to honor culinary traditions, to keep them alive, and to continue to expand our collective wisdom. And most of all, cooking is about love for the people for whom I am putting food on the table.

Cooking is an adventure, and when I am "in the groove" in the kitchen, I am relaxed and curious and happy to let my nose and my tongue lead me down unexpected culinary paths. I invite you to approach your cooking in the same manner. Play with your food!

## AN UPDATE ON LOCAL EATING

Despite the rising awareness of and enthusiasm for local foods, there is still a lot of discussion about just what "local" means. Does it entail living solely off the food we can grow and gather within one hundred miles of home, or does sourcing some ingredients from the other side of the state still "count"? Do we "allow" ourselves to continue to enjoy Parmesan cheese from Italy, coffee beans from South America, and oranges from California? Where do we draw the line, and who draws it? Perhaps what is true is that the line is continually shifting, as the needs of the earth's population change, as our resources fluctuate. We need to repeatedly reevaluate what aspects of our lifestyle in general, and our diet in particular, need to change in order to be truly sustainable.

What seems incontrovertible is that the more we acquire our food from nearby farms and streams and oceans, the more food security we will have. And truly, if we want to preserve any of the things we really need in order to thrive on this lovely planet—pure food, healthy forests, clean water, abundant fish, rich topsoil—then we must make changes in the way we value these gifts and in how we manage them. We need, as a community, to regain a sense of ownership of these resources. Getting to know your local farmers, and taking pride in saying "These vegetables were grown by my farmer!" is one step toward regaining that ownership.

A lot has happened in the culinary world since I wrote *Eating Close to Home*. Local food has become a buzzword. In many regions, fine restaurants are making a name for themselves with their ability to serve up exquisite dishes featuring locally procured ingredients. Foodie magazines such as *Bon Appétit* include tips on how to prepare in-season produce (or at least, a fruit or vegetable that is in season somewhere). The internet is loaded with bloggers writing about eating locally, and bookstores are stocked with new titles featuring recipe collections for seasonal cooking. Farmers markets are popping up like mushrooms after a good rain, and many schools are incorporating school gardens and healthy lunch programs into their curricula.

Who could have imagined, twenty years ago, that the White House would be host to an organic garden?!

This is wonderfully exciting, although in my more cynical moments I fear that local seasonal eating may turn out to be a fad for many folks, to be set down when the next great culinary idea comes along.

On the other hand, we may have little choice in the matter. Not only has the public's awareness of local food issues grown, but so, too, has our awareness of climate change and resource depletion. It has become clear to many people that we need to find alternatives to a lifestyle that is so dependent on fossil fuels, both because we are running out of the stuff, and because our continued dependence on oil is contributing to changes in our fragile planet's atmosphere that threaten to alter how we feed ourselves, whether local food continues to be the latest rage or not.

For me, shopping at a farmers market is a wonderfully hopeful activity and a great antidote for those times when I feel discouraged about what the future might hold. When I am at the market, I feel connected to my community. And I see the same response in those around me—people are engaged, excited, and buoyed up by the great abundance and incredible diversity and beauty of the fruits and vegetables on display. So whether you are interested in eating locally because doing so contributes to greater health (which it does), because local food is so wonderfully tasty (which it is), because you recognize the value in supporting local farmers (which is immeasurable), or because you have experienced the excitement and energy and satisfying sense of connection that comes from shopping at your farmers market, I hope you will join me in broadening the range of foods you source from your own region to include those of the fourth cornerstone: beans, grains, nuts, and seeds.

# BEANS, GRAINS, NUTS & SEEDS IN THE PACIFIC NORTHWEST

Worldwide, beans and grains comprise about eighty percent of what we humans eat. If you include the beans and grains used for animal feed, the amount is even higher. Unlike fresh fruits and vegetables, beans and grains are wonderfully easy to store for long periods of time, without refrigeration or processing other than a thorough drying after they are harvested. Beans and grains are highly nutritious, containing a wide range of essential minerals, amino acids, and proteins. Many varieties can be grown without extensive irrigation—a definite plus in the many areas where water resources are dwindling. And through their ability to cultivate symbiotic bacteria that "fix" nitrogen, beans actually improve the soil!

Nuts and seeds are another valuable source of protein and can also be pressed to make cooking oils. The Willamette Valley is known for its hazelnuts (filberts), but both hazelnuts and walnuts can be grown throughout the Pacific Northwest. Once established, a nut tree is a wonderfully low-input source of high-quality nutrition. Sunflower seeds can be grown in a great number of areas, and flax is very well suited for this region, too.

Most of the beans and grains currently available at the average grocery store in the Pacific Northwest were grown somewhere far afield. The grains that were ground to fill your sack of flour might have been grown in eastern Washington or eastern Oregon, but more likely, they were sourced from central Canada, the Midwest, or beyond. Wherever they were grown, they were probably shipped to yet another location to be milled, and then stored in a warehouse for some length of time. Those navy beans you just picked up off the shelf? They were most certainly not grown locally, and might be a year or two old. Your almonds and your rice probably originated in California.

Not too long ago, though, the Pacific Northwest was self-sufficient in grain production, and grain grown here supported cities along the West Coast as far away as San Francisco. Every town had a grain elevator, and many towns had mills. Washington's Skagit Valley was covered with oat fields that fed horses in the cities. Bakeries in the Puget Sound area were supplied by grain grown in the San Juan Islands. Farmers small and large grew many varieties of dried beans that were well adapted to our relatively short, cool summers.

But during the last two generations or so, the infrastructure to support and the knowledge of how to grow grains and beans has dwindled. Farmers either sold their land or turned to easy cash crops such as grass seed. The Willamette Valley, for instance, became the grass seed capital of the world—much to the dismay of those afflicted with seasonal allergies! As regional food production dwindled, the grain mills and silos were abandoned. Canneries were dismantled, and a region that was once fully capable of feeding itself became dependent on food imported from around the globe.

However, there is change afoot! Nationwide, groups of farmers are coming together to revive the once common knowledge of how to feed their communities with not just fruits and vegetables, dairy, and meats, but with beans and grains as well. The Willamette Farm and Food Coalition and the Ten Rivers Foodweb in Eugene and Corvallis, Oregon, respectively, are but two examples of people coming together to foster the movement to relocalize our food system. The Willamette Valley Bean and Grain Project, spearheaded by Harry McCormack, has been helping grass seed farmers to rediscover how to grow beans and grains. Krista Rome of the Backyard Beans and Grains Project in Whatcom County, Washington, is focusing on helping small-scale gardeners and farmers alike grow grains and beans. Washington State University at Mt. Vernon, under the direction of plant breeder Stephen Jones, is similarly involved in helping farmers to reestablish grain production. Fields of wheat—both hard red and soft white—are finding their way back to the Pacific Northwest, along with barley, oats, rye, flax, and buckwheat. Farmers are also experimenting with a multitude of heirloom dry bean varieties, along with other edible seeds such as teff, millet, flax, and quinoa. Grain mills are being rebuilt: Green Willow Mill in Brownsville, Camas Country Mill in Eugene, to name a couple.

And more people—consumers and chefs alike—are realizing not only that locally grown grains and beans are exciting because of the part they play in relocalizing our food system, but that they also bring a wonderful array of new (or renewed) flavors to our food. Just as a peach purchased from the supermarket will be but a poor imitation of a peach picked just hours before you hold it in your hand, "fresh" dried heirloom beans have a depth of flavor that you will never find in a can. And a loaf of bread, whole wheat or otherwise, made from heirloom grains will have a complexity of taste that can surprise even experienced bakers. Not only do the various types of heirloom grains differ in flavor, but grains grown in one region will taste different than those grown elsewhere—much as wine grapes from specific regions are unique.

Rebuilding our food-system's infrastructure requires resources and represents a significant capital investment for the farmers and community groups who convert their fields from grass seed to beans and grains for human consumption, build mills and dry storage facilities, reestablish distribution networks, and purchase the necessary farm equipment. We *can* feed ourselves locally, but the fledgling system needs our support. Community members can help by seeking out locally grown beans, grains, nuts, and seeds and learning to cook with them. By patronizing restaurants that use local beans and grains. By purchasing a bean and grain CSA share. By getting to know the farmers who sell their products at the market and letting them know what you enjoyed.

It is also important to remember that the availability and quality of local products is affected by the vagaries of the weather. The weather in any given region and year will affect the moisture and protein content of wheat (which changes how it will behave when you go to make a loaf of bread). Early fall rains can affect how much of the bean crop can be successfully harvested, and late spring rains can delay planting. Becoming familiar with and empathetic toward the challenges that your local farmers face on a daily basis can be tremendously supportive of them.

Pricing is another area where awareness can be increased. Large-scale industrial farms can charge much less for their products as they have the economies of scale on their side. Smaller farms, run by a family or a few individuals, must charge more. We need to be willing to pay a fair price that reflects the true cost of the product.

One of the most important things you can do is to just start cooking! Become familiar and comfortable with the routine of soaking and cooking beans and grains on a regular basis. Add them into your daily life, bit by bit, getting to know how they taste and what you like. Start small—a complete and sudden overhaul of your larder or your diet is rarely successful. But keep at it, and before you know it, beans, grains, nuts, and seeds will be a part of your life, and you will be a part of this movement!

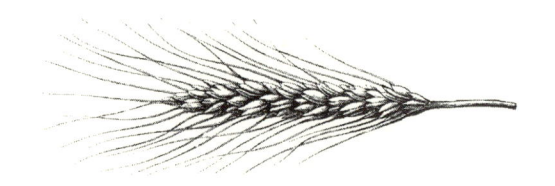

# BEANS

Beans have been a part of the human diet for centuries, and for good reason. Dried beans are an incredibly compact, easily stored vehicle for imbibing the sun's energy. They can be incorporated into a vast array of cooking styles, and what is more, they are truly good for you. Beans contain almost everything you need in your diet to keep your system functioning well: complex carbohydrates, fiber, omega-3 oils, high-quality protein, and a host of minerals and vitamins such as the B complex vitamins. That's quite a line up!

It is only recently, and largely in the U.S., that beans have been seen as less than desirable. They became associated with poverty and gained a reputation for being too hard to cook, and, more problematically, too hard to digest. In addition, there is a common misconception that cooking beans from scratch requires a great deal of time and planning—a resource that many people in our busy society lack.

The reality is that dried beans (especially dried beans that have not been sitting on a shelf for several years) can be cooked relatively quickly—not as fast as prying open a can, but still very manageably. And once you incorporate beans into your diet on a regular basis, your body will adapt, and that bowl of beans will be less likely to cause digestive discomfort.

Beans are quite the bargain, too. One pound of dried beans makes eight cups of cooked beans, which goes a long way in terms of putting meals on the table. According to the USDA, a half-cup of cooked beans provides nine grams of protein—as much as roughly two ounces of meat—half a day's fiber, and all in a low-glycemic package, which means your blood-sugar level stays stable after your meal. Not bad for a humble bean!

### WHAT BEANS ARE THESE?

The world of beans is vast and colorful. Bean varieties range from the more well-known types, such as black beans, pinto beans, navy beans, and lentils, to the more exotic heirloom beans such as Ireland Creek Annie, Jacob's Cattle, Eye of the Goat, and Good Mother Stallard (to name only a few). The internet is a great place to track down the long list of intriguing varieties and to get to know the characteristics of each. Heirloom beans are generally more flavorful and disease resistant, and their vines tend to bear and ripen over an extended period of time—an attribute which makes them less convenient for industrial-scale agriculture but well suited for small farmers.

Following is a list of some of the main families of beans we use in North America. Not all of these are grown in the Pacific Northwest. Additionally, as more heirloom or heritage-type beans are brought into the area, you may well find locally grown beans that are not listed here. (Heirloom or heritage varieties are those that have been in culture for at least fifty years.) Ask your farmer to suggest ways that they have enjoyed cooking a particular bean. Try substituting heirloom beans for the more commonly found beans in your favorite recipes.

**Black-Eyed Peas (*vigna unguiculata*).** Also called crowder pea, Southern pea, brown-eyed peas, and Black-Eyed Suzies, these legumes are often cooked with ham hocks and greens and served for good luck on New Year's Day. As it happens, they are very high in nutritional value.

**Garbanzo Beans (*cicer arietinum*)** are also called chickpeas in this country, ceci beans in Italy, and by several other names throughout the world. Canned garbanzos can be mealy and tasteless. Try a locally grown, freshly cooked garbanzo bean, and you will see what a poor imitation the canned version is! Garbanzo beans take longer to cook than other beans (45 minutes to an hour, depending on how fresh they are) and definitely do better with a soak. Sprouted garbanzo beans cook up even faster—see the directions for sprouting on page 28.

**Fava Beans (*vicia faba*).** Also called broad beans, fūl, or ful medames. Fresh fava beans are a seasonal treat in Italy and deserve to be celebrated thus in the U.S., as well. Available in the spring, young favas are great in salads. Older fava beans have a tough skin that needs to be removed before eating. Dried fava beans are earthy and chestnut-like in flavor and have a dense floury texture.

**Lentils (*lens esculenta*).** Most of us are familiar with the green and brown lentils found in almost every grocery store. But did you know there are over fifty varieties of lentils grown in India alone? Some types, such as red lentils, French green lentils, and tiny black lentils, are becoming more available in the U.S. as farmers experiment with growing different varieties. Tom Hunton of Camas Country Mills grows several and is introducing more every season. Other farmers throughout the Pacific Northwest are doing the same. Lentils are a wonderful bean to keep on hand, as they do not need to be soaked and they cook in 20 to 30 minutes.

**Lima Beans (*phaseolus lunatus*).** Large limas include the Christmas or chestnut lima bean, an heirloom variety that is becoming well known of late. Small limas are also called butter beans. Young lima beans are excellent as a fresh shelling bean and can be used instead of fresh fava beans.

**Runner Beans (*phaseolus coccineus*).** This branch of the family includes scarlet runner beans and runner cannellini beans. Popular especially in England, where they are eaten as a fresh shelling bean, they are also good as a dried bean.

And then there is the very large and sprawling family of beans called *phaseolus vulgaris* or **Common Bean**. In truth, there is nothing common about most of these beans, nor are they vulgar! The common bean includes such familiar names as kidney beans, pinto beans, navy beans, cannellini beans, and black beans. It also includes the wonderful world of heirloom beans.

Heirloom beans grown in the Pacific Northwest include:

| | |
|---|---|
| **Arikara** | **Eye of the Tiger** |
| **Borlotti** | **Flageolet** |
| **Borlotto del Valdarno** | **Hidatsa Red** |
| **Brightstone** | **Hutterite soup beans** |
| **Buckskin** | **Indian Woman Yellow** |
| **Calypso (also known as Orca or Yin-Yang)** | **Jacob's Cattle** |
| | **Koronis Purple** |
| **Cherokee Trail of Tears** | **Rio Zape** |
| **Cranberry** | **Rosso di Lucca** |
| **Dutch Bullet** | **Swedish Brown** |
| **Early Warwick** | **Yellow-Eyed** |

Increasingly, local farmers are experimenting with these older strains to select for the best flavor, and are bringing back almost-forgotten types of beans to see what grows best in their locale. While all of these beans have distinctive personalities, beans in general are very flexible and interchangeable. Try different varieties of beans for delicious new twists on basic dishes like chili and bean dip.

Fresh shelling beans are becoming common at farmers markets, and bean CSAs are joining the ranks of other community supported agricultural endeavors. This is a great time to be experimenting and including more beans in your diet!

## ABDOMINAL RUMBLINGS

Beans can be a cause of flatulence in some people. On the other hand, so can a host of other vegetables, most of which we don't as a culture shy away from. Broccoli, Brussels sprouts, cabbage, oat bran, celery, raisins, raw carrots, and milk all contain complex sugars called oligosaccharides that can be difficult for our digestive tract to break down without the assistance of helpful resident bacteria. When beans pass through our lower intestine, bacteria get to work breaking down whatever our digestive enzymes could not handle. If the right kinds of bacteria are not present, this process is limited, and gas is produced as a by-product.

The good news is that as you eat beans more regularly, your digestive system's bacterial community will adapt and become more efficient at breaking down the complex sugars. When you start adding beans to your diet, try eating small amounts to give your system time to develop better bean digesting enzymes. It is worth the effort —more and more evidence suggests that complex gut bacterial communities that are well equipped to break down plant oligosaccharides do a great deal to promote good health.

Soaking beans in water activates enzymes that enhance the beans' digestibility. A well cooked bean, one that has been cooked low and slow, will be easier to digest. I often add a square of kombu (kelp seaweed) to the pot, particularly when I am not using other seasoning. The enzymes in the seaweed aid in digestion, and kombu gives the beans a rich, somewhat elusive taste. The kombu should be rinsed briefly or wiped with a damp cloth before being added to the pot, and then removed when the beans are tender.

Adding a bay leaf, or a sprig of epazote (a Mexican herb that is particularly tasty with black beans) is also said to improve the digestibility of beans. Ginger, anise, and fennel seeds can also help, as does cumin.

# SPROUTING BEANS

Sprouting beans takes the soaking process to the next level. The enzyme changes that occur during the sprouting process make beans even easier for your system to process and also reduce the cooking time.

Beans triple in size during the sprouting process, so start with one-third of the ultimate quantity of beans you want. A large-mouth quart-size mason jar is a good sprouting vehicle for small amounts of beans. Use a lid with holes—either a commercial sprouting lid or a canning jar ring with a piece of food-grade wire mesh or nylon fabric stretched over the top. Good air circulation is essential.

Rinse and pick over the beans to make sure there is no debris. Put ½ to ¾ cup of beans in the jar and fill it with water. Cover the jar with a towel to keep it dark, and soak for 24 hours. If possible, and especially in warm weather, change the water every 12 hours.

After 24 hours, drain your beans and thoroughly rinse them two or three times. The beans now need to be kept moist, but not wet. After the last rinse, tilt the jar and set it in the dish rack or propped up a bit on the counter so the extra water drains off. Then lay the jar on its side, cover it with a towel, and set it on the counter, where you will not forget about it. The beans need to be rinsed and drained several times a day for three or four days; they'll sprout faster in warm weather than in cold.

When the tails of the beans are the length of the bean itself, but not longer than one inch, they are ready to cook. Do not wait until they have leaves!

Place the sprouted beans in a pot and cover with water. Bring to a boil, then turn down the heat, and simmer until tender, about 45 minutes to an hour. Use cooked sprouted beans as you would any other cooked bean.

# BEAN COOKING BASICS

There are four basic steps to remember when cooking beans: Sort, Soak, Season, and Simmer. Multiple variations exist within each of these steps, but if you master these four basics, you'll soon be cooking beans like a pro.

**SORT**

Start with the freshest dried beans you can find. If you are buying beans from the bulk bin in the grocery store, look for beans that are smooth and shiny, not dull and cracked or wrinkled. Locally grown beans are the best bet; chances are they were grown and harvested within the last year, and will have the most flavor and will cook the fastest.

Sort through your beans by spreading them out on a baking sheet and removing any bits of earth or chaff (shell) that might be leftover from processing. Put your beans in a large bowl or pot, fill it with cool water, and swish the beans around a bit. Skim off any bits of shell that rise to the top, then drain. Repeat this a few times.

**SOAK**

As mentioned, many people find that soaking helps make beans more easily digested, and most agree that soaking decreases the cooking time. There is also some evidence that soaking beans may make them more nutritious.

Soaking can be done overnight, it can be done while you are off at work or at play, and it can be abbreviated. When pressed for time, you can skip soaking altogether. I have experimented with cooking beans both ways, and while I prefer eating and cooking beans that have been soaked, I do on occasion find myself with no cooked beans in the freezer, a rapidly approaching dinner hour, and a recipe that revolves around beans!

Put your sorted beans in a bowl and cover them with fresh water by two inches. Leave the bowl on the counter all day or overnight. If you think of it, give the beans a swirl a few times during the soaking.

Some folks advocate changing the water halfway through the soaking period. You will see the beans begin to swell as they rehydrate.

If you haven't the time for a long soak, simply put your beans in a pot, add water to cover by two inches, and bring them to a boil. Remove from the heat, let the beans sit for an hour, then drain. This is known as the quick-soak method.

There are a few types of beans that do not require a soak: split peas, black-eyed peas, pigeon peas, and lentils.

## SEASON

You can cook beans with no seasoning at all, but I usually add at least a square of kombu or a bay leaf to the cooking water. Or, if you want to bring those beans up a notch or two, cook your beans with *soffritto*.

*Soffritto* is the Italian answer to the French *mirepoix*: the main difference being that a *mirepoix* is sautéed more gently. Either way, Italian or French, it involves a carrot, a small onion, a stalk of celery, and a handful of parsley. Mince them all finely. Add a few glugs of olive oil to the pot in which you will be cooking your beans, and warm it up. Toss in the vegetables and sauté over medium heat for 7 to 10 minutes, until the ingredients start to soften, and the onion begins to take on a bit of color. Celery, carrot, and onion are the backbone of a *soffritto*, but you could also add some chopped fennel bulb, a clove or two of garlic, or whatever other vegetables and herbs suit your fancy. If you are in a spicier mood, try adding jalapeño peppers, along with some cumin and coriander. Browning a ham hock in the pot before you add the beans is another great way add flavor.

For years, people have debated whether adding sugar, salt, or acidic substances prevents beans from becoming tender. There is some consensus that adding acid and sugar at the start of cooking does in fact result in beans that are less tender, so I add those at the end. As for salt, the jury is still out. Some cooks insist that salted beans will never become tender. Others claim that adding salt, either at the outset or halfway through the cooking time, does not result in tough beans, especially if the beans have been soaked. The age of the bean is also a factor—old beans are notorious for being tough. Try it both ways, and do what works for you! In any case, the usual ratio is a scant 2 teaspoons of salt per pound of beans.

**SIMMER**

Put your beans in a soup pot or Dutch oven and add your cooking liquid—water or broth, as you prefer. Use enough liquid to cover the beans by about two inches; generally speaking, use 4 cups of liquid per cup of beans. Turn up the heat and bring the ensemble to a boil. Once the pot has reached a boil, turn the heat down so that the beans are simmering very gently—too high a heat will cause them to burst. Partially cover the pot and go do something else for a while.

Cooking time varies greatly. Soaked beans that are less than a year old will probably be done in less than an hour. The older the bean, the longer it takes to cook. Some beans, such as garbanzo beans, require more cooking time than do, for instance, lentils, no matter how fresh they are. So while you are getting to know your beans, it is OK to hover a bit. Take a few beans out from time to time and bite into them. You want your finished beans to be tender and smooth, not hard or grainy. On the other hand, you want to take them off the heat before they fall apart or get too mushy. If you need to add more liquid to keep your beans covered, use warm water or broth so you don't shock them.

When your beans are tender, if you haven't already, add a bit of salt or soy sauce. If you eat meat, consider sautéing some bacon or ham and adding that to the pot (or cook the beans with a ham hock, as mentioned above). Give the beans 5 or 10 more minutes on the stove to absorb the flavors. Remove them from the heat, and stir in some sort of acid to round out the flavor. Citrus is great—lemon is often called for (and you can use the zest as well), but lime is fine, and oranges are fun, too. Tomatoes, either canned or fresh or in the form of tomato paste, also add acidity, as does a splash of vinegar.

After your beans are cooked, you have several choices for how to enjoy them. The most direct approach, of course, is to fill a bowl and adorn your beans with whatever toppings seem appropriate—think black beans topped with sour cream and salsa, or curried lentils topped with yoghurt mixed with mint and cucumber, or a bowl of Borlotti beans garnished with a swirl of fruity olive oil and a dusting of grated Parmesan cheese.

You can also bake your cooked beans, usually adding molasses or some sort of sugar to prevent the beans from breaking down further. You can purée or mash them, making a dip (such as hummus) or refried beans. This is an excellent way to use beans you have inadvertently cooked a bit too long. Or you can combine your beans with other ingredients to make a soup or salad or casserole.

Beans can be cooked on the stovetop in your favorite pot, where they are easily watched over and tasted along the way. They can also be cooked in a crockpot or slow cooker while you are off doing other things. There are many types of slow cookers on the market: some will cook beans in three hours or so, while others will produce finished beans overnight. Or you can use a pressure cooker and cook your beans practically at the last minute! I prefer using the pressure cooker when I am going to purée them or make refried beans, as beans cooked this way seem less inclined to hold their shape.

**COOK LOTS OF BEANS!**

Whatever you ultimately want to do with your beans, consider cooking twice as much as you need. I find it economical to soak and cook a large batch of beans on the weekend, and then utilize them in various dishes throughout the week. If covered and refrigerated immediately, cooked beans will store in their cooking liquid for up to three days.

Cooked beans can also be frozen and pulled out later for a last minute bowl of bean dip or an impromptu pot of soup. They can be frozen with or without their cooking liquid. Beans frozen in the "pot liquor" will last longer before succumbing to freezer burn and are good for recipes that call for some of the cooking liquid to be added to the dish. On the other hand, small amounts of beans frozen without liquid are great for tossing in a salad or pan of pasta. I try to keep some of each on hand.

# BEAN APPETIZERS

Lentils, black beans, white beans, garbanzos—all are wonderful when cooked and puréed for a spread or a dip. You are probably familiar with hummus and Mexican bean dips. But that is just the beginning!

If you are cooking up a batch of beans and they get away from you and start to lose their shape, don't despair! Change your plans and make a spread. If you have extra beans, toss them in the freezer, and pull them out when you need to whip up a fast appetizer or a sandwich spread. Purée the thawed beans with olive oil, some caramelized onions, salt and pepper, and perhaps a tablespoon of capers, and voilà!

For a more complex flavor, add roasted vegetables, some nut butter, and a variety of spices and herbs. Thick purées are great on crostini or bruschetta, maybe topped with some sautéed greens. Thinned with a bit of broth or olive oil, a bean purée can be tossed with hot pasta.

Of course, bean-based appetizers are not limited to dips! In this section, along with a few suggestions for bean dips and pâtés, you will find two somewhat more unusual appetizers: Ceci Fritta (page 36) and Farinata (page 38).

## ARIKARA BEAN PÂTÉ WITH TOASTED SPICES

The Arikara bean was a primary food crop for the Mandan and the Arikara Indian tribes of the Missouri Valley. These beans were among the many horticultural "discoveries" of Lewis and Clark, and perhaps more importantly, helped feed and sustain the members of their expedition through a winter of sub-freezing temperatures. Arikara beans were grown by Thomas Jefferson at Monticello, and now by many farmers in the Pacific Northwest.

**2 cups Arikara beans, sorted and soaked (see page 29)**

**2 Tablespoons olive oil**

**1 small onion, minced**

**1 bay leaf**

**1 Tablespoon cumin seeds**

**½ Tablespoon coriander seeds**

**½ teaspoon fennel seeds**

**1 teaspoon coarse salt**

**3 cloves garlic, minced**

**1 Tablespoon lemon juice**

**1 Tablespoon olive oil**

**Dash cayenne pepper**

**Chopped parsley for garnish (optional)**

Drain and rinse the soaked beans. In a large pot, heat the olive oil, and sauté the onion until soft. Add the beans, the bay leaf, and water just to cover. Bring to a boil, then reduce to a simmer, and cook, partially covered, until tender, about 45 minutes. Allow to cool. Drain, reserving the cooking liquid and discarding the bay leaf.

In a small dry cast-iron skillet, toast the cumin, coriander, and fennel seeds over medium-low heat, until they darken somewhat and the aroma intensifies. Grind the toasted spices with the salt in a spice grinder or mortar and pestle.

In a food processor, purée the garlic with the ground spices. Add the beans and enough of the reserved bean-cooking liquid to make a smooth paste. Add the lemon juice, olive oil, and cayenne pepper.

Remove to a bowl and garnish with a swirl of olive oil and, if you like, some fresh chopped parsley.

**VARIATIONS:** This spice combination is tasty with many other types of heirloom beans.

### SPICES: WHOLE OR GROUND, TOASTED OR NOT?

Fresh whole spices are packed with flavor. Ground spices can be easier and are certainly faster to work with, but their flavor fades much faster in storage, so they need to be replaced more often. To substitute ground for whole spices in a recipe, figure on one teaspoon of ground spice for one tablespoon of whole spice.

Toasting spices such as cumin, coriander, and mustard seed intensifies their flavor. Many recipes call for toasting whole spices in a dry skillet before grinding them. If you are pressed for time or don't have a spice grinder or mortar and pestle, it is possible to toast ground spices in oil or in a dry skillet as you would whole spices.

## CECI FRITTA (Fried Garbanzo Beans)

In Italy, garbanzo beans are called *ceci* (pronounced *chay*-chee). Fried in a bit of olive oil and dusted with herbs and spices, they make an easy, tasty appetizer. Alternatively, use them as you would croutons, sprinkled on a salad or a bowl of soup.

Makes about 2 cups of beans—a healthy bowlful.

**1 cup garbanzo beans, sorted and soaked (see page 29)**

**1 small square of kombu or 1 bay leaf and 1 clove garlic, peeled but whole**

**¼ cup olive oil**

**1 to 2 cloves garlic, finely minced**

**1 to 2 Tablespoons minced fresh thyme**

**1 to 2 Tablespoons minced fresh parsley**

**1½ teaspoons ground cumin**

**Salt and pepper to taste**

Drain and rinse the soaked garbanzo beans. Place in a pot with the square of kombu, or the bay leaf and peeled garlic clove. Cover with fresh water by two inches and bring to a boil. Reduce to a simmer, and cook, partially covered, until tender, about 45 minutes to 1 hour, depending on the age of the beans. (Garbanzo beans can be cooked a day or two ahead and refrigerated in their cooking liquid.)

Drain, remove the kombu or bay leaf and garlic clove, and spread the beans out to dry on paper towels or a clean tea towel.

Heat the olive oil in a large skillet over medium heat. Add the minced garlic and sauté until tender but not browned. Add the garbanzo beans and cook, shaking the pan from time to time, until they begin to pop and turn golden. Drain the beans on a paper towel, then transfer to a serving dish. Sprinkle with the thyme, parsley, and cumin. Add salt and pepper to taste. Serve warm or at room temperature.

## MEDITERRANEAN LENTIL TAPENADE

Inspired by *The Versatile Grain and the Elegant Bean*.

In this spread, cooked lentils are paired with olives, anchovies, capers, and lemon. The anchovies can be omitted for a vegetarian version. As the lentils do not need to be presoaked, this recipe comes together quickly.

Makes about 2 cups.

**1 cup green or brown lentils, sorted and rinsed**

**1 bay leaf**

**½ cup pitted Kalamata olives or other oil-cured olives, drained**

**3 to 4 oil-packed anchovy fillets (optional)**

**1 Tablespoon capers, drained**

**2 large cloves garlic, finely minced**

**1 teaspoon dried oregano**

**1 teaspoon lemon zest**

**Juice of 1 large lemon**

**¼ cup olive oil**

**1 Tablespoon chopped parsley**

In a medium saucepan, combine the lentils, bay leaf, and enough water to cover by two inches. Bring to a boil. Reduce heat, and simmer, partially covered, until the lentils are very tender, about 30 minutes. Drain, remove the bay leaf, and set aside.

In a food processor, chop the olives finely, then add the lentils, anchovies, capers, garlic, and oregano, and process until smooth. Add the lemon zest, 1 tablespoon of the lemon juice, and the olive oil, and process further, until a thick creamy purée forms. Adjust the seasonings, adding more lemon juice or olive oil, according to your taste. Serve at room temperature, sprinkled with chopped parsley, to be scooped up with your favorite crackers, bruschetta, or fresh vegetables.

## FARINATA

*Farinata* is an Italian dish native to Liguria. Garbanzo beans are ground to a fine powder and then mixed with olive oil and water and baked to resemble either a flatbread or a polenta or a frittata but really is like none of the above. Farinata can be adorned with a variety of toppings or eaten plain, either as a side dish or as an appetizer.

Serves 4 to 6.

**1 cup garbanzo bean flour — Bob's Red Mill makes one**

**1¼ cup water**

**½ teaspoon salt**

**5 Tablespoons olive oil, divided**

**½ large onion, thinly sliced (optional)**

**1 Tablespoon minced fresh rosemary, or substitute sage (optional)**

Preheat the oven to 500°F.

Whisk together the garbanzo bean flour, water, salt, and 3 tablespoons of the olive oil. The batter should be the consistency of a thin pancake batter, so if necessary, add a bit more water. Let the batter rest for at least 30 minutes.

If using the onion, sauté it with a sprinkling of salt, in a skillet over medium heat until it is golden. Set aside.

Add about half a tablespoon of olive oil to a 10- to 12-inch skillet and swirl to coat. Place the skillet in the oven and heat it for 5 to 10 minutes, until very hot. Carefully remove from the oven and add a cup of batter. If you are using them, scatter a bit of the onion and the rosemary or sage over the top, and return to the oven. Bake 15 minutes or more, until the farinata begins to set. Now turn the broiler on and broil for an additional 5 minutes or so, until the top is golden brown and the sides look as if they are getting crispy.

Remove to a cutting board. Make the second farinata in the same manner, preheating the pan for 5 minutes before adding each cup of batter.

Let the farinata rest for a few minutes before cutting into wedges or squares.

For a thinner, crispier farinata, use a bigger skillet with less batter (¼-inch deep). For a creamier farinata, more like polenta, pour in enough batter so that it is ½-inch deep, or use a slightly smaller skillet.

You can top your farinata with cooked pancetta, chopped olives, thinly sliced and sautéed vegetables, crumbled cheese, or whatever suits your fancy.

Leftover farinata is good cut into chunks and tossed with salad.

### MORE FUN WITH FARINATA

Try adding ½ cup of flour (whole wheat or white) plus 1 teaspoon of baking powder to the garbanzo-bean flour and salt. In a separate bowl, beat 2 eggs and mix in ⅓ cup olive oil and ½ cup warm water. Whisk the wet ingredients into the dry and let the batter rest. Pour into a greased 8-inch cast-iron skillet and bake at 425°F, for 25 to 30 minutes. This savory cake can be adorned with tomatoes, grated cheese, or other such toppings before going into the oven.

## IRELAND CREEK ANNIE BEAN BRUSCHETTA

Contributed by Karen Guillemin.

Ireland Creek Annie beans are an English heirloom variety grown since the 1930s on Ireland Creek Farm in British Columbia. As a contrast to this rich and pungent spread, try the Red Pepper Sauce layered onto the Bruschetta.

Makes about 3 cups of Bean Spread.

### BEAN SPREAD

**2 cups cooked Ireland Creek Annie beans (see page 29)**

**5 to 6 cloves garlic, whole and unpeeled**

**¼ cup olive oil**

**Salt to taste**

Roast the garlic cloves in a dry skillet, until the skin is blackened in spots and the garlic is soft. Peel the garlic and combine it with the cooked beans and olive oil in a food processor. Blend until very smooth. Add salt to taste.

### BRUSCHETTA

**1 baguette, sliced on the diagonal**

**Olive oil**

Preheat the broiler. Spread a thick layer of Bean Spread onto each baguette slice, followed by a stripe of Red Pepper Sauce. Lightly coat an oven-safe skillet with olive oil, and heat it on the stove on medium-high heat. Add the bruschetta to the pan, and let them cook for a minute to toast the bottom of the bread. Then put the pan under the broiler for about 5 minutes, until the edges of the bruschetta are toasted.

**VARIATION:** The Bean Spread, topped with a layer of Red Pepper Sauce if you wish, also makes a nice dip for raw vegetables or toasted pita triangles.

## RED PEPPER SAUCE FOR BRUSCHETTA

**1 red pepper**

**⅓ cup almonds**

**½ teaspoon smoked paprika**

**1 Tablespoon red wine vinegar**

**Salt to taste**

Char the red pepper over an open flame or cut in half and roast (cut side down) on a baking sheet in a 400°F oven, until the skin is blackened. Place in a bowl and cover with a plate to steam off the skin. Toast the almonds, then chop coarsely in a food processor. Scrape the charred skin from the pepper, remove the stem and seeds, and add to the food processor. Add the paprika and vinegar, and process into a coarse paste.

## WINTER WHITE BEAN DIP WITH TURNIPS, LEMON & SAGE

Adapted from *The Versatile Grain and the Elegant Bean*.

Tangy and creamy, this unusual combination of beans and turnips makes good use of winter vegetables. Choose a bean with a smooth consistency, such as Arikara, Dutch Bullet, cannellini, or Hutterite soup beans.

Makes about 2½ cups.

**1 cup white beans of your choice, sorted and soaked (see page 29)**

**1 small onion, peeled and stuck with a few whole cloves**

**1 small turnip, peeled**

**1 small carrot**

**1 small stalk celery**

**1 large clove garlic**

**1 bunch parsley**

**1 bay leaf**

**¼ teaspoon red chile flakes**

**2 Tablespoons lemon juice**

**1 to 2 teaspoons lemon zest**

**3 fresh sage leaves, minced**

**¼ cup olive oil**

**1 teaspoon salt**

**½ teaspoon pepper**

Drain and rinse the soaked beans. Place in a pot with fresh water to cover, along with the onion, turnip, carrot, celery, and garlic clove. Tie the parsley and bay leaf in a square of cheesecloth, and add to the pot along with the red pepper flakes. Bring to a boil, then reduce to a simmer and cook, partially covered, until the beans are very soft, about 45 minutes. Remove from heat and drain the beans, reserving the turnip and the garlic.

Purée the beans, turnip, and garlic in a food processor until smooth. Transfer to a bowl, and add the lemon juice and zest, sage, olive oil, salt, and pepper. Serve at room temperature with raw vegetables, crackers, or crostini.

**VARIATION:** Rutabaga or celeriac could be used in place of (or in addition to) the turnip.

### CROSTINI OR BRUSCHETTA?

Both are toasted bread used in Italian cooking as canvases for a wide variety of toppings. But what is the difference?

Crostini ("little toasts" in Italian) are thin slices of grilled or toasted bread, usually a small, round, fine-textured type of bread such as a white flour baguette. Crostini are often spread with intensely flavored toppings such as olive tapenade, goat cheese with fig jam, or sautéed chopped wild mushrooms.

Bruschetta is typically made from a larger, more rustic loaf of bread, which is cut into thick slices and often toasted over the embers of a fire (*bruscare* means "to roast over coals"). The toasted bread is then rubbed with a clove of garlic, drizzled with olive oil, and sprinkled with salt. Bruschetta is often served with chopped ripe tomatoes and basil, cannellini bean purée, or sautéed greens and garlic.

# JUST A BOWL OF BEANS, PLEASE

Sometimes a simple bowl of beans—accompanied by a bit of bread, maybe a few olives or other pickled things, and a glass of wine to wash it all down—is all that is needed on a cold, rainy afternoon! Let those winter winds blow! Of course, a bowl of beans topped with juicy, fresh tomatoes makes a great supper in the summer, as well.

Following are a few recipes that feature bean cuisine from several different regions. You'll find beans cooked with Italian flavors, Indian spices, and French herbs. Give them a try, and then start playing with your own favorite herb and spice combinations.

### LEMON-WALNUT CILANTRO SAUCE FOR YOUR BEANS

A dab of traditional Basil Pesto (page 227), a bit of Parsley Pesto (page 79), Spanish Sofrito Sauce (page 55), or Lemon-Walnut Cilantro Sauce will wake up a bowl of plain beans. Sauces and pestos are also great swirled into bean soup.

**1 cup cilantro, thick stems removed**

**¼ cup parsley**

**2 cloves garlic**

**½ cup walnuts**

**⅓ cup fresh lemon juice**

**¼ teaspoon ground cumin**

**1 teaspoon salt**

**Olive oil as needed**

Combine all ingredients in a food processor. Thin with olive oil to the consistency you prefer. Use fresh, or freeze in small amounts, such as in an ice cube tray.

**VARIATIONS:** Add a cup of fresh mint leaves and/or ½ cup of fresh basil.

## DANIEL'S BLACK BEANS

Adapted from a recipe by Daniel Klein from The Perennial Plate website.

These deeply flavorful beans are cooked with a sachet of seasonings that includes smoked tea. Wonderful served straight from the pot to your bowl, they are just as good leftover and made into pancakes or puréed for a dip.

Serves 6 to 8.

**2 cups black beans, such as Cherokee Trail of Tears, sorted and soaked (see page 29)**

**5 cups water or stock**

### THE SACHET

**¼ teaspoon smoked cayenne pepper flakes, or 1 small red chile**

**3 large cloves garlic, peeled**

**1 large bay leaf**

**1 small stick cinnamon**

**1 Tablespoon toasted coriander seeds**

**1 teaspoon toasted cumin seeds**

**1 Tablespoon whole black peppercorns**

**1 teaspoon Lapsang Souchong tea leaves, or other smoked tea such as Russian Caravan**

**4- to 6-inch square of butter muslin or cheesecloth**

Drain and rinse the soaked beans and place in a pot with the water or stock. Place the sachet ingredients in the center of the butter muslin or cheesecloth, draw up the corners to form a sachet bag, and tie with a piece of kitchen twine. Nestle this in the middle of your pot of beans. Bring to a boil, then reduce to a simmer, and cook, partially covered, about 45 minutes, until the beans are tender. Remove the bag of seasonings, add salt to taste, and serve.

## BEANS WITH PESTO AND PISTOU

Beans are just as wonderful tossed with pesto as is pasta! Following are two variations on a theme of pesto and beans. Both can be made with fresh shelling beans instead of dried beans, in which case there is no need to soak.

### BEANS WITH BASIL PESTO

Serves 4 to 6.

**1½ cups Cranberry or Borlotto del Valdarno beans, sorted and soaked (see page 29)**

**1 bay leaf**

**2 Tablespoons Elin's Basil Pesto (see page 227)**

**1 Tablespoon lemon juice**

**3 Tablespoons olive oil**

**Salt and pepper to taste**

Drain and rinse the soaked beans and place in a pot with the bay leaf. Cover with fresh water by two inches and bring to a boil. Reduce to a simmer, and cook, partially covered, until tender, about 45 minutes. Discard the bay leaf.

Drain the beans and transfer to a bowl. While still warm, toss with the pesto, lemon juice, olive oil, and salt and pepper to taste. Serve immediately.

## BEANS WITH TOMATO PISTOU

In this version, beans are tossed with a tomato pistou—a French pesto made with tomato paste.

Serves 4 to 6.

**1½ cups Cranberry or Borlotto del Valdarno beans, sorted and soaked (see page 29)**

**1 bay leaf**

**2 cloves garlic, peeled and coarsely chopped**

**½ teaspoon salt or to taste**

**1½ cups basil leaves**

**⅓ cup olive oil, plus extra for serving**

**½ cup Parmesan cheese, grated**

**3 Tablespoons tomato paste**

Drain and rinse the soaked beans and place in a pot with the bay leaf. Cover with fresh water by two inches and bring to a boil. Reduce to a simmer, and cook, partially covered, until tender, about 45 minutes. Discard the bay leaf.

In a bowl, mash the garlic and salt with the back of a wooden spoon until smooth, or use a mortar and pestle if you have one at hand. Place the basil and olive oil in a food processor, and buzz it a few times to make a rough purée. Add the garlic and salt mixture, the grated cheese, and the tomato paste and blend until combined. Taste and add more salt, if you like.

Drain the beans and transfer to a bowl. While still warm, toss with the pistou. Serve with an additional swirl of olive oil.

## BRAISED ROSSO DI LUCCA BEANS WITH ROSEMARY AND THYME

Rosso di Lucca beans are rich and delicious and marry well with strong flavored herbs such as rosemary and thyme. They are grown in the Willamette Valley by Open Oak Farm from beans collected by a seed preservation group in Tuscany, Italy. Other white beans, particularly Cranberry or Borlotti beans, work just as well.

Serves 4 to 6.

**2 cups Rosso di Lucca beans, sorted and soaked (see page 29)**

**3 sprigs fresh rosemary, divided**

**2 sprigs fresh thyme**

**1 bay leaf**

**2- to 4-inch piece of Parmesan rind**

**¼ to ½ cup olive oil, divided**

**1 medium yellow onion, chopped**

**4 cloves garlic, minced**

**¼ cup balsamic or red wine vinegar or a mixture**

**Salt and pepper to taste**

Drain and rinse the soaked beans. Place in a pot and cover with fresh water by two inches. Add 2 sprigs of the rosemary, the thyme, and the bay leaf (you can tie them up in a piece of cheesecloth for easy retrieval), along with the Parmesan rind. Bring to a boil, then reduce to a simmer, and cook, partially covered, until tender but not mushy, 45 minutes or more, depending on the age of the beans. Add more water (room temperature) if necessary to keep the beans covered.

Remove from heat, discard the herbs and the Parmesan rind, and stir in 2 tablespoons of the olive oil and salt to taste. Let the beans sit a bit to cool and absorb the salt, or cover and chill overnight in the cooking liquid.

In a 3-quart Dutch oven or braising pan, heat ¼ cup of olive oil over medium heat. Add the onion and cook, stirring occasionally, until translucent. Add the garlic and sauté a few minutes longer. Drain the beans, reserving a cup of the bean liquor.

Add the beans and the reserved bean liquor to the onions and garlic. (If you've refrigerated the beans, heat them gently before adding them to the pot.) Add the remaining sprig of rosemary and the vinegar. Bring to a boil, then decrease the heat, and simmer until the liquid has been reduced and is dark and syrupy, about 15 minutes.

Add salt and pepper to taste. Remove the rosemary, drizzle with more olive oil, and serve. Pass grated Parmesan cheese at the table.

**VARIATION:** After cooking the beans, put the sautéed onions, beans, and so forth in a bean pot and bake for 1½ to 2 hours at 325°F. Let cool for 30 minutes before serving.

## CALYPSO BEANS WITH COCONUT MILK, GINGER & BLACK MUSTARD SEEDS

Adapted from a recipe by Karen Guillemin.

Calypso beans are also known as Orca beans or Yin-Yang beans because of their markings—white with black splotches. The texture and taste is somewhat like that of a russet potato. Cooking them in coconut milk results in a luscious, creamy bowl of beans.

Serves 6 to 8.

**2 cups (1 pound) calypso beans, sorted and soaked (see page 29)**

**1 yellow onion, chopped**

**2 Tablespoons olive oil**

**1-inch piece ginger root, minced**

**5 cloves garlic, minced**

**2 teaspoons ground cumin**

**2 teaspoons ground coriander**

**14-ounce can coconut milk**

**2½ cups water**

**Salt to taste**

**Cilantro**

**Simple Tarka**

In a large, heavy-bottom soup pot or Dutch oven, sauté the onion in olive oil until golden.

Drain and rinse the soaked beans, then add them to the pot along with the ginger, garlic, spices, coconut milk, and water. Bring to a boil, reduce to a simmer, and cook, partially covered, until the beans are tender, about 45 minutes. Alternatively, cook in a slow cooker on low for about three hours.

Stir the Tarka into the beans and serve. Pass a bowl of chopped fresh cilantro at the table.

> **SIMPLE TARKA**
>
> **1 Tablespoon butter or vegetable oil**
>
> **1-inch piece ginger root, peeled and finely diced**
>
> **1 teaspoon black mustard seeds**
>
> Heat the butter or oil and sauté the ginger and mustard seeds over medium-low heat for a few minutes, until the mixture is fragrant.

> **WHAT IS TARKA?**
>
> Tarka is a cooking technique originating in India and Pakistan and other nearby countries in which spices are added to very hot oil. Heating the spices intensifies the aroma and flavor, which are retained by the oil, making tarka an excellent means of delivering an extra punch to a dish. Tarka can be added at the beginning of the cooking process, as is common in making curry, or at the end, as with dal or stew. Common ingredients include onion, garlic, fresh ginger, dried chile, fresh curry leaves, cumin seed, coriander seed, fenugreek seed, nigella seed, black mustard seed, and green or black cardamom pods.

## NABIHA'S FATHER'S WAY WITH LENTILS (Chanay Ki Daal)

Originally from Pakistan, Nabiha was a colleague of mine at the Oregon Bach Festival. This is her father's recipe for preparing lentils.

Serves 4 to 6.

**1½ cups green or red lentils, or yellow split peas, sorted and rinsed**

**3 cups water**

Rinse the lentils well. Put the lentils and water in a large soup pot, bring to a boil, then reduce heat and simmer, partially covered, until tender but not falling apart. With the back of a spoon or a potato masher, mash some of the lentils to thicken the mixture.

Season the lentils with:

**¾ teaspoon salt**

**⅛ to ¼ teaspoon cayenne pepper or to taste**

**¼ teaspoon turmeric**

And add to the pot:

**1 to 2 fresh tomatoes, chopped, or use canned**

**¼ cup tomato sauce**

**1 cup chopped cilantro or more to taste**

Add more water to thin if desired, and simmer for another 15 minutes or so, until the flavors are well acquainted.

In the meantime, make the Tarka.

Add the Tarka to the lentils, and garnish with additional fresh cilantro and fresh chopped tomatoes (if in season) just before serving.

**VARIATIONS:** Nabiha says her aunt also sprinkled garam masala on the beans when serving. I like a squeeze of lime juice at serving time.

### NABIHA'S FATHER'S TARKA

¼ to ½ cup oil

1 onion, halved and sliced thinly

¼ teaspoon black mustard seed

½ teaspoon cumin seed

¼ teaspoon coriander seed

1 to 2 teaspoons minced fresh ginger

1 to 2 teaspoons minced garlic

¼ or more teaspoon cayenne pepper flakes, or minced fresh green chiles (optional)

In a frying pan, heat the oil and add the onion. Sauté for a few minutes, until the onion begins to soften, then add the black mustard, cumin, coriander, ginger, garlic, and cayenne pepper or fresh chiles (if using). Sauté for a few more minutes, until the seeds darken and the aroma is heady.

## SLOW-ROASTED TOMATOES

This is not a recipe, really, just an outline of yet another way to capture the essence of summer in a jar. Delicious with your bowl of beans, tossed with hot pasta, folded into a grain salad, or spread on Polenta Crostini (page 132). Whatever you don't eat immediately can be stored in a jar in the refrigerator or frozen for mid-winter delight.

**Ripe tomatoes, halved and seeds removed, if you prefer**

**Olive oil**

**Whole cloves garlic, unpeeled (optional)**

**Chopped fresh herbs, such as basil, parsley, rosemary, or thyme (optional)**

**Salt and pepper**

Preheat the oven to 300°F. Arrange the tomatoes cut side up on a baking sheet (you can line it with parchment paper for easier clean up). Don't crowd the tomatoes — you want the air to be able to circulate. Tuck the garlic cloves (if using) around them. Drizzle liberally with olive oil. Sprinkle with chopped fresh herbs, if you are using them, and a bit of salt and pepper.

Bake for 2 hours or so, until the tomatoes are shriveled and fairly dry but still have a bit of juice inside. The exact timing will depend on the type of tomato and their size. When done to your satisfaction, remove the tomatoes to a jar or storage container, discarding the garlic or herbs. Top with olive oil and store in the refrigerator or freezer.

A note about the temperature: It's not written in stone. 300°F for 2 hours, 225°F for 3 hours, 400°F for 1 hour — it all works.

## SPANISH SOFRITO SAUCE

This thick, jammy, intensely flavored sauce turns up in various forms in Spain, Latin America, the Caribbean, and points in between. There are hundreds of variations, but all result in a sauce that is excellent as the base for a soup or stew, tossed with pasta, spread on bread, or as a topping for a bowl of beans.

Makes 2 cups of sauce.

**½ cup olive oil**

**1 small onion, minced**

**2 large cloves garlic, minced**

**1 teaspoon chopped fresh rosemary**

**¼ teaspoon red pepper flakes**

**1½ teaspoons smoked Spanish paprika**

**4 cups paste tomatoes, chopped — peeled and seeded, if you prefer**

**2 large, roasted red peppers — jarred peppers are fine**

**Salt and pepper to taste**

**1 teaspoon balsamic or red wine vinegar**

Heat the olive oil in a large saucepan or deep skillet. Add the onion and sauté over medium heat, until it begins to brown. Add the garlic, rosemary, and red pepper flakes and cook another minute or two, until the garlic softens. Add the paprika, then immediately add the tomatoes and peppers. Bring to a boil, then reduce heat to a simmer.

Cook over medium-low heat for about an hour. The tomatoes will give off a lot of juice, which will reduce to a thick sauce. Stir from time to time to keep the sauce from sticking to the pan. At some point, the oil will separate from the sauce and will be a beautiful red color. That is when the sauce is done. Season with salt and pepper and a teaspoon or so of vinegar.

**VARIATIONS:** Chopped green olives or capers can be added along with the tomatoes and peppers or at the end of the cooking time.

# BEANS AND MORE

On occasion, you might want something a bit fancier for dinner than just a pot of beans. Perhaps your father-in-law is coming for dinner, and he doesn't consider a meal without meat to be a meal at all. Of course, you can pair any of the bean recipes in the preceding section with a roast of some sort, or throw something on the grill, or add some browned sausages. Following are a few ideas for combining beans and meat, as well as a few vegetarian main dish ideas that raise the humble bean to more elevated levels.

### A COMPOSED BOWL

The easiest way to "fancy up" a batch of beans is to compose a bowl. Start with your choice of cooked grain for the foundation. Brown rice, quinoa, barley, or couscous are all good candidates. Ladle a serving of cooked beans over the grains. Now strew a liberal helping of steamed, roasted, or raw vegetables on top. Crown your bowl with pesto, salsa, or another sauce. Dust with Dukkah (page 230), Furikake (page 231), grated cheese, yoghurt, or sour cream as the occasion requires. Dig in!

## ARIKARA BEANS WITH TOMATILLO PORK

Slightly modified from a recipe contributed by Karen Guillemin.

This makes a wonderful meal when accompanied by Pickled Onions and a slaw of carrots, red peppers, radishes, and lightly pickled cabbage (pages 58 and 59). Other pinto-type beans (such as Eye of the Tiger) can replace the Arikara beans.

Serves 6 to 8.

**2 cups Arikara beans, sorted and soaked (see page 29)**

**1½-pound boneless pork roast**

**2 Tablespoons Worcestershire sauce, or more as needed**

**1 Tablespoon neutral oil such as grapeseed or canola**

**1 pound fresh tomatillos, husked and cut into chunks**

**1 bunch cilantro, minced**

**6 cloves garlic, coarsely chopped**

**4 to 6 pickled jalapeños, coarsely chopped**

**1 fresh jalapeño, seeded and coarsely chopped (optional)**

**Salt to taste**

Liberally rub Worcestershire sauce on all sides the pork. Heat the oil in a deep pot and sear the pork until it starts to brown, on all sides. Remove from heat and put the pork in a slow cooker. Add the tomatillos, cilantro, garlic, and the pickled and fresh jalapeños to the slow cooker, and cook on high for about three hours.

Remove the pork to a plate. Use an immersion blender to purée the vegetables into a smooth sauce. Drain and rinse the soaked beans. Add the beans and, if needed, enough water to ensure that all the ingredients are submerged. Add the pork back to the slow cooker and cook on low for another three hours, until the beans are soft.

Remove the pork and shred with a fork. Salt the beans to taste. Stir the shredded pork back into the beans and keep warm. Serve on warm tortillas with Crunchy Slaw and Pickled Onions.

## TWO ACCOMPANIMENTS

For your Arikara Beans with Tomatillo Pork… or any other bowl of beans!

### PICKLED ONIONS

**1 large onion, sweet Walla Walla onions are wonderful, purple onions lend a lovely fuchsia color**

**¼ teaspoon cumin seeds**

**¼ teaspoon coarse salt**

**⅛ teaspoon ground black pepper**

**1 small bay leaf**

**Pinch of dried oregano or a few fresh oregano leaves, minced**

**2 to 3 cloves garlic, lightly crushed but left whole for easy retrieval**

**⅓ cup cider vinegar**

Slice the onion as thin as you can—an eighth inch or less if possible. Bring a small saucepan of water to a boil and add the onion. Blanch the onion in the water for a minute or so to temper the pungency. Drain and remove to a serving bowl. (You can skip this step if you are using a sweet onion or don't mind the sharper flavor of a purple onion.)

Toast the cumin seeds and grind them coarsely with a mortar and pestle or in a spice mill. Add the cumin, salt and pepper, bay leaf, oregano, garlic, and vinegar to the onions, along with enough water to cover. Stir and let the onions marinate for several hours or longer. Remove garlic cloves if desired.

Keep leftovers covered in the refrigerator. Great with sandwiches, too.

## CRUNCHY CABBAGE, CARROT & RADISH SLAW

½ Savoy cabbage, cored and finely chopped

3 limes, divided

⅓ cup rice vinegar

1 teaspoon sugar

¼ teaspoon red pepper flakes

¼ teaspoon salt

2 carrots, cut into 1-inch long matchsticks

12 radishes, topped, tailed, and sliced into thin half-moons

1 red bell pepper, thinly sliced lengthwise and cut into thirds

1 handful of chives, minced

3 Tablespoons olive oil

Salt to taste

Smoked Ancho chile powder (optional)

In a small saucepan, combine the juice of 2 of the limes, the rice vinegar, sugar, red pepper flakes, and salt to taste. Heat until the sugar and salt dissolve. Pour over the chopped cabbage, mix, and allow the cabbage to pickle for a few minutes while you prepare the other vegetables.

Combine the carrot, radish, red pepper, chives, the juice from the remaining lime, olive oil, and salt to taste.

When you are ready to serve the slaw, stir the carrot-radish-pepper mixture into the pickled cabbage. Adjust seasoning to taste. If desired, dust the top with smoked Ancho chile powder.

## CANNELLINI BEANS WITH FRESH GRILLED TUNA

I like to make this in the summer, when wild albacore are running just off the Oregon Coast, and tomatoes are ripe and luscious.

Serves 4 to 6.

### THE BEANS

**1 cup cannellini beans, sorted and soaked (see page 29)**

**1 small onion, stuck with several whole cloves**

**1 small carrot**

**1 stalk of celery, or a bundle of celery leaves**

**1 bay leaf**

**1 handful parsley sprigs**

Drain and rinse the soaked beans. Place in a large pot, along with the onion with cloves, the carrot, and the celery. Cover with fresh water by two inches. Tie the parsley (and celery leaves, if using) with kitchen twine, and add that and the bay leaf to the pot. Bring to a boil, then reduce to a simmer, and cook, partially covered, until tender, about 45 minutes. Add salt to taste during the last 3 minutes. Drain the beans, discard the vegetables, and set aside to cool.

### THE TUNA

**1 pound tuna loin, or tuna steaks or another full-flavored fish**

**Zest of one large lemon**

**2 Tablespoons of fresh rosemary leaves — about 3 good-size sprigs**

**Large handful of flat-leaf parsley**

**3 cloves garlic, crushed**

**1 teaspoon coarse salt or to taste**

**Black pepper**

**¼ cup olive oil**

While the beans are cooking, marinate the fish. Place the lemon zest in the middle of a cutting board. Pile the rosemary leaves and parsley on top, then add the garlic cloves, followed by the coarse salt and a few good twists of freshly ground pepper. Mince all of this together, until it is well macerated, then remove to a small bowl. Stir in the olive oil, then adjust seasoning, adding more salt, pepper, herbs, or lemon juice as you prefer. Add more olive oil if needed to make a paste, then rub the paste all over the tuna, and let it sit for half an hour.

Grill the tuna. When the fish is cool enough to handle, remove the skin (if using loin), and break into large bite-size pieces.

## THE SALAD

**1 small cucumber, roughly chopped**

**2 cups halved cherry tomatoes, or 2 to 3 large tomatoes, cubed**

**¼ cup chopped pitted Kalamata or other flavorful olives**

**Flat-leaf parsley, chopped**

**Assorted greens — lettuce, spinach, arugula**

## THE VINAIGRETTE

**Juice of 1 large lemon**

**1 Tablespoon white wine vinegar**

**1 teaspoon Dijon mustard**

**¼ cup olive oil**

**Salt and pepper to taste**

In a large bowl, whisk together the vinaigrette ingredients. Toss the cucumber, tomatoes, and olives with the vinaigrette, and add salt and pepper to taste.

Add the beans and tuna pieces and toss gently. Tear the greens into bite-size pieces and make a nest of greens on each dinner plate. Mound the bean and tuna mixture in the center, sprinkle with parsley, and serve at room temperature.

## ROASTED GARBANZOS WITH GARLIC AND GREENS

Adapted from *Bon Appétit* magazine.

Cooked garbanzo beans are roasted in olive oil with garlic and fennel seeds, then tossed with sautéed greens and served over rice or cooked grains.

Serves 4 to 6.

### THE BEANS

**3 cups cooked garbanzo beans (see page 29)**

**8 to 10 cloves garlic, peeled but left whole**

**2 small bay leaves**

**1 teaspoon fennel seeds**

**¼ to ½ cup olive oil**

### THE GREENS

**2 Tablespoons olive oil**

**3 cloves garlic, minced**

**½ cup chopped onion**

**Pinch of red pepper flakes**

**1 pound greens: Swiss chard, spinach, or kale, center ribs removed and cut into short ribbons**

**1 to 2 Tablespoons lemon juice**

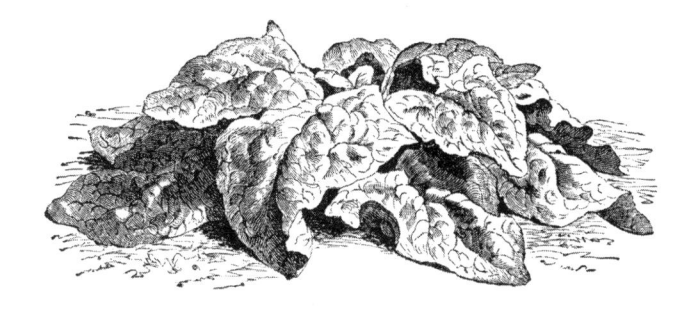

**PREPARE THE BEANS:** Preheat the oven to 350°F. Combine the cooked garbanzo beans, garlic cloves, bay leaves, and fennel seeds in a glass baking dish. Add the olive oil and toss to coat. Cover dish with foil and roast, until the garlic is tender, about 45 minutes.

**PREPARE THE GREENS:** Heat the oil in a large pot, and add the minced garlic, onions, and red pepper flakes. Sauté until the garlic and onions are soft but not browned. Add the greens and cook until wilted (kale will take longer than chard or spinach). Season with salt and pepper to taste.

**ASSEMBLE THE DISH:** Drain the garbanzos and garlic, reserving the oil and discarding the bay leaves. In a large skillet, add 2 tablespoons of the reserved oil along with the roasted garbanzos and the greens. Toss well over medium heat until warmed through, adding more of the flavored oil as desired. Season with salt and pepper and the lemon juice. Serve with rice or other cooked grains.

Any remaining oil can be refrigerated and used for other purposes!

## CRANBERRY BEANS SIMMERED WITH SAGE, SAUSAGES & TOMATOES

Serves 4 to 6.

### THE BEANS

1 pound Cranberry beans, or use Borlotti or another firm bean, sorted and soaked (see page 29)

1 sprig fresh sage

3 to 4 large cloves garlic, peeled but left whole

2 Tablespoons olive oil

1 teaspoon salt

¼ teaspoon black pepper

### THE SAUSAGES AND TOMATOES

2 Tablespoons olive oil

4 cloves garlic, minced

1 pound sweet Italian sausages, cut into rounds

1 small onion, minced

1 stalk celery, minced

1 carrot, minced

2 cups chopped paste tomatoes—canned, fresh, or frozen

2 large sprigs fresh sage

**PREPARE THE BEANS:** Drain and rinse the soaked beans and place in a large pot, along with the sage and garlic. Cover with fresh water by two inches and bring to a boil. Reduce to a simmer, and cook, partially covered, until tender but not falling apart, about 45 minutes. Add the olive oil, salt, and pepper, and let the beans cool in the cooking liquid. When cool, remove the garlic and the sage. Drain, reserving ½ cup of the bean liquor.

**PREPARE THE SAUSAGES AND TOMATOES:** Heat the olive oil in a large skillet, add the garlic and sauté until golden. Add the sausages and sauté until they are browned on each side. Remove the sausages to a plate. Sauté the onions, celery, and carrot in the skillet until soft (add another splash of olive oil if needed). Add the ½ cup of reserved bean liquor, the tomatoes with their juices, and the sage. Simmer until the tomatoes have broken down.

**ASSEMBLE THE DISH:** Add the sausages back to the pan along with the beans and 1 cup of water. Cover and simmer, until the sausages and beans are warmed through, about 30 minutes. Uncover and simmer until the sauce is thickened. Season with salt and pepper.

Good served on top of polenta and dusted liberally with grated Parmesan cheese.

**VARIATIONS:** If you prefer, the sausages can be omitted. Or add 2 to 4 cups of packed, shredded kale leaves (or other greens) to the skillet after you sauté the onions, carrots, and celery.

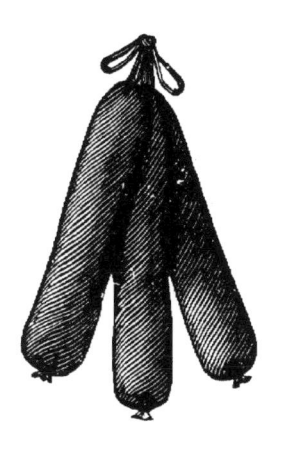

## JOANNA'S CHILI

A modified version of a family favorite, using locally grown kidney beans such as Brightstone (grown by Open Oak Farm in Sweet Home, Oregon). Angostura bitters, a good beer, and lots of spices make this a very special chili.

Serves 6 to 8.

**2 cups Brightstone or other kidney beans, sorted and soaked (see page 29)**

**½-pound round steak or other lean cut, trimmed and cut to a fine dice**

**1 large onion, coarsely chopped**

**1½ pounds tomatoes, canned, frozen, or fresh—if using canned, crush them with your hands; if frozen, slip the skins off in a bowl of warm water; if fresh, chop coarsely**

**1½ cups tomato purée**

**3 Tablespoons aromatic bitters—Angostura bitters or Swedish bitters**

**3 Tablespoons Worcestershire sauce**

**1 bottle good-quality beer—a nice hoppy IPA works well**

**3 cloves garlic, minced**

**½ to 1 teaspoon red pepper flakes**

**2 bay leaves**

**1 Tablespoon chile powder**

**1 teaspoon ground coriander**

**1 teaspoon ground cumin**

**1 teaspoon thyme**

**1 teaspoon oregano**

Drain and rinse the soaked beans and place in a pot. Cover with fresh water by two inches and bring to a boil. Reduce to a simmer, and cook, partially covered, until tender, about 45 minutes. Drain and set aside.

In a large soup pot or Dutch oven, brown the meat over medium heat. Add the onion and cook until soft. Stir in the remaining ingredients and the beans. Bring to a boil, reduce heat, and simmer uncovered, stirring occasionally, until the chili is thick and the flavors are well acquainted. Remove the bay leaves.

Serve with shredded cheddar cheese, sour cream, chopped cilantro, fresh lime, and/or fresh salsa.

### THE GREAT CHILI DEBATES

Chili or chile—which is the seasoning and which is the dish? The question continues to be debated hotly, and the answer depends on where the expert you consult lives. The word chile comes from an Aztec word, *chil*, meaning pepper. The Spanish added an "e" to make a noun in their language. So what about the word ending in "i"? Generally, in most parts of the U.S., the consensus is that Chile is the country in South America, chile is the pepper, and chili is the dish consisting of beef, chiles, and (sometimes) beans.

Which leads us to the other incendiary question of whether beans are allowed in chili (the dish). Serious chili aficionados (a great many of whom reside in or come from Texas), insist that real chili is made only from meat and chiles (the hot pepper). Adding beans to the pot only dilutes it, making it more palatable to babies and the elderly, and is technique generally practiced by Yankees. However, since the International Chili Society's World Chili Cook-Off now includes a chili-with-beans division, it may be that you can add beans to your pot, as I do, in good conscience.

BEANS AND MORE

## MEDITERRANEAN-STYLE PASTA AND BEANS

I thought originally of calling this Beans and Snails, as I like making it with the Italian pasta called *chiocciole*, which means "snail." It could also be called Beans and Ears, as it is equally good with *orecchiette* (Italian for "little ears"). Of course, if *farfalle* pasta is used, the dish could be named Beans and Butterflies (*farfalle* means "butterfly" in Italian). Whatever you call it, and whatever shape pasta you choose, it is a lovely summer dish when zucchini and cherry tomatoes are in abundance, and equally good with sun-dried tomatoes and broccoli in the winter.

Serves 6 to 8.

½ pound pasta

1 small onion, diced

3 Tablespoons olive oil, plus extra for serving

3 to 4 cloves garlic, minced

¼ teaspoon red pepper flakes

2 to 3 medium zucchini, sliced lengthwise in quarters and then into ½-inch slices

1 sweet red pepper, diced

2 cups cherry tomatoes—red or yellow or a mixture—halved

2 cups cooked white beans of your choice—cannellini, white emergo, Arikara, Indian Woman Yellow all work well (see page 29)

1 teaspoon fresh oregano or ½ teaspoon dried oregano

½ cup or more minced parsley

¼ cup minced fresh mint

Zest of one lemon

½ to 1 cup crumbled feta cheese

½ cup roughly chopped pitted Kalamata olives

Bring a large pot of salted water to a boil, and cook the pasta until *al dente*.

While the water is coming to a boil, in a large skillet, heat the olive oil and add the onion. Cook over medium heat until the onion is soft and translucent. Add the garlic and red pepper flakes, and cook another minute or two. Add the zucchini and red pepper, and cook until the vegetables begin to soften. Add the tomatoes, beans, and oregano, and cook until the tomatoes break down and are saucy, about 5 minutes.

By this time the pasta should be done. Add the pasta and a ladleful of the pasta water to the vegetables. Toss in the parsley, mint, and lemon zest, and let the ingredients simmer for a few minutes while the pasta absorbs some of the sauce.

Pour the ensemble into a pasta bowl and gently fold in the feta cheese and olives. Drizzle olive oil over the top and serve.

**VARIATIONS:** Add a bunch or two of roughly torn spinach or chard leaves to the pan when you add the pasta. Kale is also good but needs more time to cook, so add it with the zucchini. Leave out the pasta and serve on top of rice or polenta for a gluten-free meal.

## BLACK BEAN, CHORIZO & RICE STEW
## WITH CILANTRO AND TOASTED PUMPKIN SEED SAUCE

Contributed by Katherine Deumling from the Cook With What You Have website.

Serves 6 to 8.

1½ cups black beans, sorted and soaked (see page 29)

4 ounces fresh bulk chorizo or smoked chorizo sausages, chopped

2 Tablespoons olive oil

1 medium onion, diced

1 large carrot, diced

2 to 3 cloves garlic, minced

1 teaspoon ground cumin

5 or more cups water or broth

½ cup long- or short-grain brown rice

½ teaspoon kosher salt

Black pepper to taste

Cilantro and Toasted Pumpkin Seed Sauce (see page 72)

Heat a large soup pot or Dutch oven over medium-high heat. Add the chorizo and cook until browned. If using bulk chorizo, break it up as it cooks. Remove the chorizo to a plate, and add the oil to the pot along with the onion, carrot, and garlic. Cook, stirring occasionally, until the vegetables begin to soften, 5 to 10 minutes. Add the ground cumin and the browned chorizo back to the pot.

Drain and rinse the soaked beans, and place in a pot with the broth or water. Bring to a boil, reduce to a simmer, and cook, partially covered, for 20 minutes.

Add the rice and kosher salt and cook for another 30 to 40 minutes, stirring occasionally. If the rice and the beans have absorbed all of the liquid but are not yet completely cooked, add up to a cup more warm liquid and continue cooking a bit longer, until the rice is tender.

Serve the stew in bowls with a healthy spoonful of Cilantro and Toasted Pumpkin Seed Sauce (page 72) on top. Pass more sauce at the table.

**VARIATIONS:** If you prefer not to use chorizo, omit it but brown the onions well for added depth of flavor. And, along with the cumin, add a teaspoon of smoked paprika.

Pinto beans would work well in lieu of black beans.

This stew is very nice accompanied by roasted winter squash with Ancho chile powder. Cut a butternut or other meaty winter squash into 1-inch cubes. Toss with a few good slugs of olive oil, a sprinkling of coarse salt, and a teaspoon or more of smoked Ancho chile powder. Spread on a rimmed baking sheet and cook at 375°F, for 20 to 30 minutes, until the squash is tender and starting to caramelize. You can serve the squash on the side, or sprinkle it on top of the stew as you would croutons.

For a slightly more elegant presentation, you can cook the rice separately, ladle the black beans over it, and garnish with the sauce. This stew is even better if you can let it sit for a while and then reheat it.

## CILANTRO AND TOASTED PUMPKIN SEED SAUCE

This sauce is so addictive that you'll likely put it on many other things. You can use it as a salad dressing, toss it with roasted potatoes or squash, stir it into scrambled eggs, serve it over rice with chopped avocado and green onions, etc.

Makes about 1½ cups.

**1 to 2 jalapeño, Anaheim, or poblano chiles, roasted directly over your gas burner or under the broiler until blackened, peeled and seeded**

**4 Tablespoons pumpkin seeds or sunflower seeds, roasted 15 to 20 minutes in a 300°F oven or toasted in a dry skillet — be careful they don't burn**

**2 cups packed cilantro leaves and stems**

**1 large clove garlic, chopped**

**¼ teaspoon or more salt**

**2 Tablespoons good olive oil**

**1½ Tablespoons red or white wine vinegar or cider vinegar**

**1 Tablespoon lime juice**

**½ cup Greek or plain whole-milk yogurt**

**¼ teaspoon ground cumin**

Add all ingredients to the food processor or blender and blend until smooth. Taste and adjust seasoning. You can add water if it's too thick. It will thicken up a bit in the fridge as it sits. The flavor improves after sitting for a while so try to make it an hour before using, but don't let that stop you from making it if you don't have the time.

**VARIATION:** You can omit the chiles and substitute a little cayenne or red pepper flakes to simplify this recipe.

# BAKED BEANS

Some people have very firm opinions about bean pots and the type of beans one should bake in them. My mother, for instance, informs me that, in a pot of Boston baked beans, Maine Yellow-Eyed beans are equal to none. And they taste better, I am told, if baked in a true bean pot. These are deep, big-bellied ceramic pots with a fairly narrow mouth and thick walls that keep the bean liquid from evaporating too fast and allow for a long, slow cook. In the U.S., we associate bean pots with Boston, but in fact, many cultures have their own pots in which they bake beans. Mexican *olla* pots and Indian *handi* are two such vessels, and perhaps were the original inspiration for the Boston bean pot.

In any case, it is quite possible to bake beans without a proper bean pot. A cast-iron Dutch oven works just fine. And many types of beans can be baked. Adding some form of sugar to the beans allows them to bake and absorb more flavor over a long period of time without breaking down—and allows the cook to go off and do other things while the beans bake.

## EUNICE'S YELLOW-EYED BAKED BEANS

This recipe is similar to the one my grandmother used. My mother says that when she was growing up in Massachusetts, almost every Saturday night there was a baked bean supper, which invariably included baked beans, coleslaw, Boston brown bread, assorted homemade pickles and relishes, and sometimes, frankfurters. Sunday morning breakfast frequently consisted of buttered toast with reheated beans on top. White beans or navy beans can be used instead of Yellow-Eyed beans.

Serves 6 to 8.

**1 pound Yellow-Eyed beans, sorted and soaked (see page 29)**

**¼ pound lean salt pork (optional)**

**3 Tablespoons brown sugar**

**¼ cup dark molasses**

**¼ cup catsup**

**2 Tablespoons tomato paste**

**1 Tablespoon Dijon mustard**

**1 Tablespoon dry mustard**

**½ teaspoon ground ginger**

**1 onion, stuck with 2 whole cloves**

Drain and rinse the soaked beans and place in a soup pot. Cover with fresh water by two inches and bring to a boil. Reduce to a simmer, and cook, partially covered, until tender, about 45 minutes, depending on the age of the beans. Drain the beans, reserving the bean liquor.

If you are using salt pork, score it into ½-inch squares and slice off the rind. While the beans are cooking, simmer the salt pork in a small pot of water for about 15 minutes.

Transfer the beans to a bean pot or Dutch oven. Mix in the brown sugar, molasses, catsup, tomato paste, mustards, and ginger, and nestle the onion down in the center of the beans. Place the salt pork (if using) on top, partially submerged, with the scored side up. Add just enough of the bean liquor to barely cover the top of the beans.

Cover and bake at 275°F for 6 hours. Check periodically and add more of the bean liquor if necessary. Remove the lid during the last 45 minutes or so to let the beans brown a bit.

**VARIATIONS:** If you prefer not to use salt pork, sauté 4 slices of thick, meaty bacon until thoroughly cooked but not crispy. Chop roughly and add to the bean pot. If you prefer no meat at all, instead of adding the onion whole, chop it and sauté it slowly in olive oil until golden brown. If you don't have a bean pot, you can use a crockpot or slow cooker (this is a good way to make baked beans in the summer when you don't want to have the oven going). Just put everything in the pot, turn it on high until the beans begin to bubble, about 30 minutes, then reduce to low, and cook for 6 to 8 hours.

## CHOCOLATE BAKED RIO ZAPE BEANS

The list of ingredients is a tad lengthy and, with coffee and chocolate, somewhat unusual, but the flavors balance each other very well, and the result is a deeply satisfying pot of beans.

Serves 6 to 8.

**1 pound Rio Zape beans or other pinto beans or black beans, sorted and soaked (see page 29)**

**1 bay leaf**

**1 teaspoon cumin seeds**

**1 small dried chipotle chile, split open and seeded — or substitute 1 canned chipotle chile with 1 teaspoon of the Adobo sauce**

**1 Tablespoon chile powder**

**1 teaspoon dried oregano**

**1/8 teaspoon cinnamon**

**2 Tablespoons olive oil**

**1 medium onion, chopped**

**2 to 4 cloves garlic, chopped**

**2 roasted chile peppers of your choice — I use Anaheim, but you can use something with more heat — seeded and chopped**

**1 ounce very dark chocolate, finely chopped (about 3 Tablespoons)**

**2 cups canned whole tomatoes, chopped, with their juice, or equal amount of roasted tomato sauce**

**1 cup very strong coffee**

**Boiling water or stock as needed**

Drain and rinse the soaked beans and place in a large pot. Cover with fresh water by two inches, add the bay leaf, and bring to a boil. Reduce to a simmer, and cook, partially covered, until tender, about 30 to 45 minutes, depending on the type of bean and how fresh it is. Remove the beans from the heat. Discard the bay leaf and drain, reserving the bean liquor.

While the beans are cooking, heat the cumin seeds over low heat in a dry cast-iron skillet, until they start to pop and smell toasty. Cool briefly, then combine the cumin seeds and the dried chipotle chile (if using) and buzz in a spice or coffee grinder until finely ground. Transfer to a small bowl, mix in the chile powder, oregano, and cinnamon, and set aside.

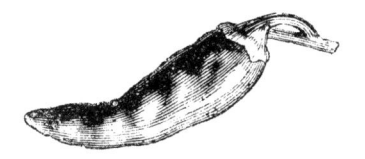

Add the olive oil to the skillet and sauté the onions over medium-high heat until softened. Add the garlic and cook for another minute. Add the chile-spice mixture and cook, stirring, for 30 seconds.

Place the onion-spice mixture in a bean pot or Dutch oven. Stir in the roasted peppers, chocolate, tomatoes, coffee, and the beans. If you are using a canned chipotle chile, add it at this point. Pour in the reserved bean liquor until it barely covers the beans. If there is not enough liquid, add water or stock. Stir gently until just combined.

Cover the pot and bake at 275°F for 6 hours. Check every few hours to make sure the liquid level is maintained.

Serve with chopped cilantro, sour cream or yoghurt, salsa, cornbread or tortillas or rice, grated cheddar or jack cheese.

## FARMOR'S BRUNA BÖNAR (Swedish Baked Beans)

These beans were always part of our Christmas Eve smörgåsbord. They were served with the hot foods, accompanied by *köttbullar* (Swedish meatballs) and *limpa* (Swedish rye bread). I've seen some recipes in which a cinnamon stick was added to the pot along with the molasses, vinegar, and butter, but the following recipe is the one passed on from my great-grandmother (also named Elin) to my father's mother.

Serves 6 to 8.

**2 cups Swedish brown beans, sorted and soaked (see page 29)**

**5 Tablespoons molasses**

**4 Tablespoons cider vinegar**

**2 Tablespoons butter**

**1 teaspoon salt**

**2 teaspoons cornstarch, made into a smooth cream with a bit of water**

Drain and rinse the soaked beans and place in a large pot. Cover with fresh water by two inches and bring to a boil. Reduce to a simmer, and cook, partially covered, until tender, about 30 minutes to 1 hour, depending on the age of the beans.

When the beans are just tender, add the molasses, vinegar, butter, salt, and cornstarch. Simmer for another 15 minutes, so the beans can absorb the flavors.

Remove from heat and cool. If possible, let the beans sit in the refrigerator for a few days to allow the flavors to develop. Bake in a casserole dish or bean pot in a low oven (300°F or so) for one hour or more, until the beans are bubbling and the sauce has thickened.

# PATTIES, BURGERS & OTHER TASTY CAKES

People have been making patties, burgers, croquettes, cakes, fritters, and a myriad of other variations on a theme from leftover beans and/or grains for a very long time. What, after all, is falafel, but a Middle Eastern version of a bean burger? I prefer my patties topped with a tasty sauce of some sort and presented on a bed of greens, rather than enclosed in a bun, but buns are great for those occasions when you need a hearty meal.

The basic outline for a bean burger is this: Mash or purée your leftover beans, add seasonings, grains, or breadcrumbs, an egg to hold the dough together, and perhaps a bit of cooked vegetables for pizzazz. Work into a dough, divide the dough into balls, and flatten them. Fry them carefully in a non-stick or well-seasoned cast-iron skillet, or if you prefer, bake in the oven. Patties can be rolled in cornmeal or breadcrumbs for an extra crunchy coating. Frying them in larger amounts of oil also results in a very crispy finish, but also adds significantly to the fat and calorie content.

### PARSLEY PESTO FOR PATTIES

**2 cups parsley**

**1 Tablespoon mint leaves**

**2 cloves garlic**

**6 Tablespoons grated Parmesan cheese**

**⅓ cup olive oil**

**Salt to taste**

Combine all ingredients in a food processor. Thin with additional olive oil to the consistency you prefer. Use fresh, or freeze in small amounts, such as in an ice cube tray.

## CRANBERRY BEANS & RYE PATTIES WITH SAGE & WALNUTS

Hearty Cranberry beans marry well with nutty rye berries, complemented by sage and toasted walnuts.

Makes 8 to 10 patties.

**1½ cups cooked Cranberry beans, or other beans of your choice (see page 29)**

**2 cups cooked rye berries, or another whole grain of your choice (see page 111)**

**4 Tablespoons olive oil, divided**

**½ cup minced shallots or red onion**

**½ cup walnuts, roughly chopped**

**1 Tablespoon minced fresh sage leaves**

**1 teaspoon dried thyme**

**2 teaspoons lemon zest**

**½ teaspoon salt**

**½ teaspoon ground black pepper**

**1 large egg, beaten**

**½ cup grated Parmesan cheese**

**Whole wheat panko or toasted breadcrumbs**

Heat 1 tablespoon of the oil in a skillet over medium heat, and add the shallots and walnuts. Sauté for about 2 minutes, until the shallots are tender and translucent. Add the minced sage, thyme, lemon zest, salt, and pepper. Mix well, then remove from the heat.

In the bowl of a food processor, combine the cooked Cranberry beans and rye berries, egg, Parmesan cheese, and sautéed shallot mixture. Process until blended into a dough that still retains a bit of texture.

Form ½-inch thick patties, and roll them in the panko. The dough will be somewhat sticky, and it may help to dampen your hands before forming the patties.

Heat the remaining oil in a large skillet. Gently transfer the patties to the skillet and cook over medium heat, for 5 to 7 minutes, until browned and crisp. Turn the patties over and cook another 4 to 5 minutes. You may need to do this in batches, and depending on what kind of skillet you use, you may need more oil to keep the patties from sticking.

Keep warm in a low oven until you are ready to serve. These are good on a bed of greens with a simple vinaigrette. They are also tasty with a tangy condiment such as Spanish Sofrito Sauce (page 55).

### HOMEMADE PANKO

Panko is a Japanese-style breadcrumb traditionally used for making deep fried foods such as tempura and *tonkatsu*. It is made from bread without the crust, coarsely ground into large airy flakes. Panko stays crispier longer because it doesn't absorb as much oil as other types of breadcrumbs.

You can make panko at home, and you can leave the crusts on if you like! Cut your bread (whole wheat or otherwise) into 2- to 3-inch strips, and put them through the feeder tube of a food processor equipped with a coarse shredder. Spread the bread shreds on a baking sheet, and bake at 300°F, for 6 to 8 minutes, shaking the pan every few minutes. The crumbs should be crisp but not browned.

## HOMEMADE FALAFEL

Until recently, I had never made falafel from scratch. Doing so was a revelation! They are not hard to make, and the flavor (not surprisingly) wildly surpasses that of the boxed falafel mix. I like to form the dough into patties instead of balls, as they need less oil to cook. Falafel are excellent served with pita bread, lettuce, fresh tomatoes, and Lemon-Garlic Tahini Sauce or Tzatziki, or both.

Makes 8 to 10 patties.

**2 cups cooked garbanzo beans (see page 29)**

**3 Tablespoons tahini**

**1 large egg**

**Lemon zest from 1 large lemon**

**1 large clove garlic, finely minced**

**1 Tablespoon lemon juice**

**1½ teaspoons ground cumin**

**¼ teaspoon turmeric**

**1 teaspoon ground coriander**

**¼ teaspoon cayenne pepper**

**½ teaspoon salt**

**¼ cup all-purpose flour**

**2 Tablespoons finely chopped onion**

**¼ cup minced parsley**

**½ teaspoon baking powder**

**Oil for frying — olive or other vegetable oil**

In a food processor, pulse together the garbanzos, tahini, egg, lemon zest, garlic, lemon juice, cumin, turmeric, coriander, cayenne pepper, and salt, until smooth but still somewhat chunky. Add the flour, onion, parsley, and baking powder, and pulse a few more times. Chill the mixture for an hour (or make ahead and keep refrigerated).

Form 1-inch thick patties, using about ¼ cup of dough for each. Place the patties on a baking sheet or large platter, keeping them separated so they don't stick together. It is helpful to dampen your hands when forming the patties.

Pour oil to a depth of ¼ inch into a large, heavy-bottomed skillet (cast-iron is great). Heat the oil over medium heat. Place several patties in the skillet, giving each a little room, and cook until golden brown on each side, about 3 minutes. Remove to a paper towel-lined platter, and keep warm while you cook the next batch.

### LEMON-GARLIC TAHINI SAUCE

**½ cup tahini**

**½ cup plain yoghurt**

**1 small clove garlic, finely minced or crushed**

**1 to 2 Tablespoons lemon juice**

**Dash each: cayenne and paprika**

**½ teaspoon ground cumin**

**Salt to taste**

In a medium bowl, mix all ingredients well with a whisk. Adjust seasonings to taste.

### TZATZIKI

**1 cup plain yoghurt**

**2 Tablespoons chopped cilantro**

**1 Tablespoon lemon juice**

**2 Tablespoons cumin**

**1 small clove garlic, finely minced or crushed**

**1 small cucumber, peeled and chopped—seeded if you prefer**

Mix all ingredients, and let stand for 15 minutes or so to allow the flavors to become acquainted.

## BEAN BURGERS WITH GREENS 'N GRAINS

If you have some cooked beans and grains stashed in the freezer, these burgers come together in a snap.

Makes 10 to 12 burgers.

1½ cups cooked beans of your choice—garbanzo beans, white beans, black beans (see page 29)

2 cups cooked grains—millet makes a light burger, rice is nice, barley is good, too (see pages 111–113)

3 Tablespoons olive oil

1 small onion, finely chopped

1 large carrot, minced

1 stalk celery, minced

1 large clove garlic, minced

1½-inch piece of fresh ginger, grated

1 teaspoon salt

⅛ to ¼ teaspoon red pepper flakes

4 to 6 cups packed greens—chard, kale, spinach, or a mixture—center ribs removed and cut into short ribbons

1 egg, beaten

1 teaspoon ground cumin

¼ cup minced parsley

1 teaspoon lemon zest

Dash of tamari

Whole wheat panko or homemade breadcrumbs

Oil for frying

Heat 1 tablespoon of oil in a skillet and add the onion. Sauté for a few minutes, until the onion softens, then add the carrot and celery. Cook for 3 minutes, stirring often, until the carrot is tender. Add the garlic, ginger, salt, and red pepper flakes, then after a few more minutes, the greens. Cover and cook for a few minutes, until the greens have wilted, then remove to a large bowl.

In the bowl of a food processor, combine the beans and grains along with the egg, cumin, parsley, lemon zest, and tamari. Process until fairly smooth but not so much that it turns into a paste. Add the sautéed greens and combine well.

Form the dough into golfball-size balls and flatten to patties. Place the panko or breadcrumbs in a shallow bowl or plate. Carefully press both sides of each patty into the crumbs.

Heat the remaining oil in a large skillet. (A non-stick skillet is great for cooking these burgers, but a seasoned cast-iron pan works just as well.) Gently transfer the patties to the skillet and cook over medium heat, for 5 to 7 minutes, until browned and crisp. Turn the patties and cook another 4 to 5 minutes. You may need to fry the burgers in batches, and depending on what kind of skillet you use, you may need more oil to keep them from sticking.

Keep warm in a low oven until you are ready to serve. Serve on a bun, accompanied by the condiments of your choice, or on a bed of greens with a dollop of plain yoghurt.

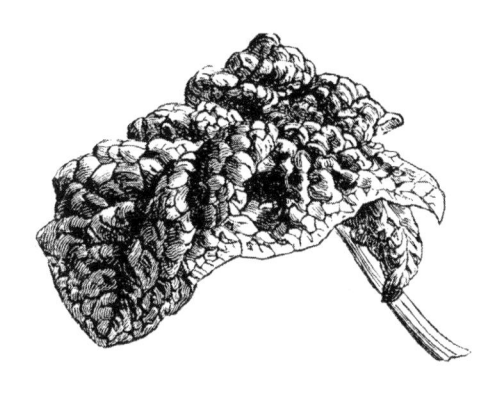

## BLACK BEAN PATTIES

Daniel's Black Beans (page 45) are wonderful in this recipe, but any cooked black bean will work.

Makes 9 to 12 patties.

**2 cups cooked black beans (see page 29)**

**1 Tablespoon tomato paste**

**1 egg, lightly beaten**

**¼ small onion, minced**

**1 to 2 cloves garlic, minced**

**½ cup dried breadcrumbs, or substitute ½ cup cooked quinoa or other grain (see page 111)**

**1 roasted chile, minced—I like Anaheim chiles**

**½ teaspoon ground cumin**

**1 teaspoon chile powder**

**1 teaspoon smoked paprika**

**1 teaspoon balsamic vinegar**

**Salt and pepper to taste**

**2 Tablespoons cornmeal—fine or medium grind, not coarse**

**Oil for frying**

**Sour cream**

**Fresh salsa**

**Cilantro**

If the beans were refrigerated (this is a great way to use leftover black beans), warm them gently. Place the beans in a large bowl and mash with a potato masher until most are broken down but a few remain whole. Add the tomato paste, egg, onions, garlic, breadcrumbs, roasted chile, cumin, chile powder, paprika, vinegar, and salt and pepper to taste. Mix well. Refrigerate dough for 20 minutes.

Cover a baking sheet with a piece of waxed paper and spread the cornmeal on it. Take a golfball-size scoop of dough in your hand, gently roll it into a ball, and then flatten it. Dip each patty in the cornmeal to lightly coat each side.

Heat enough oil to cover the bottom of a large skillet over medium-low heat. When the oil is hot, gently, using a spatula, lift each patty, and slide it into the skillet. Fry for 4 to 5 minutes on each side, adjusting the heat as necessary to keep the patties from burning but hot enough to get them well browned. Drain on paper towels and keep warm until ready to serve. Top each patty with sour cream or yoghurt, Quick Tomatillo Salsa, and cilantro.

**VARIATIONS:** Add ½ cup of pumpkin purée or mashed, roasted squash to the dough. You can also add up to a cup of leftover brown rice to complement the protein in the beans.

### QUICK TOMATILLO SALSA (Salsa Verde)

**1 pound tomatillos, husks removed**

**¼ cup chopped onion**

**1 large clove garlic, minced**

**2 jalapeño peppers, stemmed, seeded, and chopped**

**½ cup cilantro leaves**

**1 Tablespoon lime juice**

**Salt to taste**

Sear the tomatillos in a cast-iron skillet until browned on all sides, or simmer in water until soft. Add the tomatillos, onion, garlic, jalapeño peppers, cilantro, and lime juice to a food processor and pulse until finely mixed. Add salt to taste. Let the salsa rest for 30 minutes to allow the flavors to develop.

# BEAN SALADS

Beans are wonderful in salads. Throw a handful of cooked beans into a tossed green salad together with some chopped, hardboiled eggs and a few croutons, and suddenly you've got yourself a main meal. Beans and grains pair up happily to make a room temperature salad in the winter. Try beans with fresh tomatoes, still warm from the sun, and diced cucumber and sweet bell peppers, along with lots of basil and parsley and some lemon zest for an excellent impromptu salad in the midst of summer. Experiment with various combinations of fresh herbs, oils, vinegars, and citrus, and have fun!

A few rules of thumb for creating wonderful bean salads. If you have cooked your beans ahead of time, warm them and drain them well before dressing them in a salad. You will need to dress the beans with more vinegar than you may be accustomed to using in a green salad, as the beans will absorb a lot of flavor. Try a 2 to 1 ratio of vinegar to oil, and add more vinegar before serving if necessary. Serve bean salads within two hours of putting them together, and if possible, do not refrigerate them. If you must refrigerate the salad, be sure to bring it back to room temperature before serving.

## BASIC BEAN SALAD

This is not your standard issue delicatessen bean salad!

Serves 6 to 8.

**1 pound beans—good options are Indian Woman Yellow, Borlotti, cannellini, or Cranberry beans—sorted and soaked (see page 29)**

**1 bay leaf and/or other aromatics**

**¼ cup vinegar**

**1 clove garlic**

**1 teaspoon Dijon mustard**

**⅔ cup olive oil**

**2 to 3 sweet red, green, or yellow peppers, or a mixture, finely chopped**

**½ cup minced parsley**

**¼ to ½ cup minced sweet onion, or 3 scallions, chopped**

**Salt and pepper to taste**

Drain and rinse the soaked beans and place in a pot. Cover with fresh water by two inches. Add the bay leaf and/or whatever other aromatics you want. Bring to a boil, then reduce to a simmer, and cook, partially covered, until tender, about 45 minutes. Drain and remove the bay leaf.

Whisk together the vinegar, garlic, mustard, and olive oil. Toss the warm beans with the dressing, and mix in the chopped peppers, parsley, and onion. Add salt and pepper to taste.

## BEAN SALAD WITH WHEAT BERRIES AND QUINOA

Adapted from a recipe by Karen Guillemin.

Karen's recipe calls for garbanzo beans, but other firm beans can be used instead. Borlotti, flageolet, Indian Woman Yellow, scarlet runner, and cannellini beans would all hold up well. The beans and the wheat berries can both be cooked ahead of time and warmed gently before composing the salad.

Serves 6 to 8.

**1 cup garbanzo beans or other beans of your choice, sorted and soaked (see page 29)**

**1 cup wheat berries, or substitute barley or rye berries, sorted and soaked (see page 111)**

**1 bay leaf**

**¾ cup quinoa**

**1 stalk of broccoli**

**½ cup almonds, roughly chopped**

**Juice of 1 large lemon**

**2 Tablespoons sherry vinegar**

**¼ cup olive oil, plus 1 Tablespoon for toasting the nuts**

**1 teaspoon smoked paprika, plus extra for toasting the nuts**

**1 to 2 roasted red peppers, cut into small pieces**

**1 stalk celery, minced**

**1 cup kale, center ribs removed and cut into short ribbons**

**½ cup flat-leaf parsley**

**Salt and pepper to taste**

Drain and rinse the soaked beans and place in a pot. Cover with fresh water by two inches, add the bay leaf, and bring to a boil. Reduce to a simmer, and cook, partially covered, until tender but not mushy, about 45 minutes. Remove the bay leaf, drain the beans, and set aside.

Drain the soaked wheat berries. Place them in a pot with 2½ cups of water, bring to a boil, reduce to a simmer, and cook, covered, until tender but not falling apart, about 45 minutes. Drain and set aside.

Place the quinoa in a small pot with 1½ cups water, bring to a boil, reduce to a simmer, and cook, covered, for about 15 minutes, until the quinoa releases its curlicues and the water is absorbed.

Cut the flowers off the broccoli stalk, and cut the larger ones into bite-size pieces. Peel the stalk, cut lengthwise, then dice. Bring a pot of salted water to a boil, and blanch the broccoli, until tender but still bright green. Drain and set aside.

Heat a tablespoon of olive oil in a small skillet and add the almonds. Toast over medium-high heat, and when almost done, add about a teaspoon of smoked paprika and a sprinkling of salt.

In a large bowl, whisk together the lemon juice, vinegar, olive oil, and another teaspoon of smoked paprika. Add the grains and combine well with the dressing (warm the ingredients if they have been cooked ahead of time). Now add the garbanzo beans, broccoli, red pepper, celery, and kale ribbons, along with the parsley. Taste and adjust seasonings.

## GARBANZO BEAN SALAD WITH SUMMER HERBS

Garbanzo beans, lemon, and garlic are always a happy combination. Adding fresh summer herbs only improves matters.

Serves 6 to 8.

**1 cup garbanzo beans, sorted and soaked (see page 29)**

**1 bay leaf**

**Juice and zest from 1 large lemon**

**2 to 3 Tablespoons fruity olive oil**

**¼ cup chopped fresh basil**

**¼ cup chopped parsley**

**1 large clove garlic, finely minced**

**½ cup grated Parmesan cheese**

**Salt and pepper to taste**

Drain and rinse the soaked garbanzo beans and place in a pot. Cover with fresh water by two inches, add the bay leaf, and bring to a boil. Reduce to a simmer, and cook, partially covered, until the beans are tender but not falling apart, about 45 minutes. Discard the bay leaf and drain well.

Meanwhile, whisk together the lemon juice and olive oil. Add the fresh herbs and garlic.

When the beans are done, combine them in a bowl with the dressing and the Parmesan cheese. Toss gently. Add the lemon zest and season with salt and pepper to taste. If you make this ahead of time and refrigerate it, be sure to bring the salad back to room temperature before serving.

Excellent with wedges of sun-warmed tomatoes.

## SPRING BEAN SALAD

This salad is a celebration of the time of year when the sun has returned long enough to coax the early herbs out of the ground and the chickens are again laying in abundance. Of course you can make it other times of the year as well!

Serves 6 to 8.

**2 cups cooked firm beans, such as Borlotti, Cranberry, or cannellini (see page 29)**

**1 to 2 small fennel bulbs**

**4 Tablespoons olive oil**

**1 Tablespoon red wine vinegar**

**1 Tablespoon lemon juice**

**1 teaspoon Dijon mustard**

**1 small shallot, finely minced**

**½ cup hazelnuts, toasted**

**2 to 3 hard-boiled eggs, chopped**

**½ cup minced fresh spring herbs such as chervil, tarragon, chives, and parsley**

**Parmesan cheese to taste**

**Fresh spring greens**

**Salt and pepper to taste**

Remove the outer layers of the fennel bulbs, cut the bulbs in half, and cut out the tough stem. Cut in half again, and slice very thin.

Whisk together the olive oil, vinegar, lemon juice, mustard, and shallot. Season to taste with salt and pepper.

Combine the beans, fennel, hazelnuts, and eggs with the dressing and the herbs. Scatter grated Parmesan cheese over the salad, and serve on plates mounded with fresh spring greens. Pass extra Parmesan if desired, and more olive oil to drizzle as well.

# BEAN SOUPS AND STEWS

Bean soups of all kinds are found the world over. Soup just seems a natural outcome when you are cooking up a pot of beans. Like salads, bean soups are a blank canvas just waiting for your creative touch. Swirl a spoonful or two of pesto—basil (page 227), cilantro (page 44), arugula (page 169), or parsley (page 79)—into each bowl to really wake up your soup. Try a few of these recipes and see what you like, then improvise to your heart's content!

### RAITA FOR CURRIED LENTIL SOUP

1 cucumber

1 cup plain yoghurt

¼ cup minced fresh mint leaves

**Salt and pepper**

**Dash of cumin (optional)**

Grate the cucumber, using the large holes of a box grater, and set in a colander to drain. Press to extract as much water as possible. In a small bowl, combine the yoghurt, mint leaves, and cucumber. Season to taste with salt and pepper, and a dash of cumin, if you like.

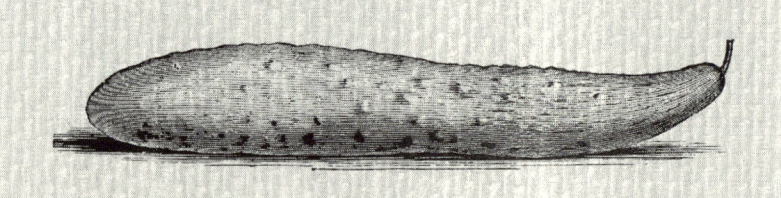

## CURRIED LENTIL SOUP

Serves 4 to 6.

**1 Tablespoon olive oil**

**1 medium onion, chopped**

**1 medium carrot, finely chopped**

**2 cloves garlic, minced**

**2 Tablespoons finely minced fresh ginger**

**1 teaspoon each: ground cumin, coriander, and turmeric**

**2 teaspoons black mustard seeds, or substitute yellow mustard seeds**

**Scant ¼ teaspoon ground cayenne pepper**

**1 cup Tom Hunton's Crimson lentils, or substitute another type**

**4 cups water or broth**

**Possible garnishes: lemon wedges, chopped cilantro, olive oil, butter, Raita (see page 94)**

In a heavy soup pot, heat the olive oil over medium heat. Add the onion and carrot, and cook, stirring occasionally, until the onion is translucent. Add the garlic and ginger, and cook another 4 minutes, until all the vegetables are softened. Add the spices and stir until they release their fragrances, about 1 minute. Add the lentils and the water or broth. Increase heat and bring to a boil, then reduce to simmer, and cook until the lentils are tender, about 30 minutes. Season to taste with salt. If you prefer, thin with a bit more liquid. If you like a smoother texture, purée in a food processor.

Serve your soup with lemon wedges and chopped cilantro. Some people like a swirl of olive oil or a pat of butter. When cucumbers are in season, Raita makes a fine accompaniment.

**VARIATIONS:** Serve with a scoop of short-grain brown rice or brown basmati rice. Add a can of coconut milk at the end of the cooking time. Or, if you are pressed for time or have a limited spice cupboard, substitute 2 to 3 tablespoons of curry powder for the mix of spices.

## LATE SUMMER LENTIL STEW WITH ROASTED VEGETABLES

This stew could be made just as easily with other beans such as Hutterite soup beans, although you would need to soak them overnight and increase the cooking time a bit. If, at the end of summer, you roast a pan or two of tomatoes and eggplant and freeze them, you can have late summer all winter long!

Serves 6 to 8.

**2 cups lentils, sorted and rinsed**

**3 pounds paste tomatoes, halved**

**1 large eggplant, peeled and cubed**

**3 to 4 cloves garlic, peeled but left whole**

**4 Tablespoons olive oil, divided**

**1 medium onion, diced**

**3 stalks celery, diced**

**1 large carrot, diced**

**1 teaspoon powdered mustard**

**½ teaspoon ground cumin**

**½ teaspoon ground coriander**

**1 large bay leaf**

**4 cups stock or water**

**Salt and pepper to taste**

**Lemon juice (optional)**

Preheat the oven to 425°F.

In a large, rimmed baking sheet or roasting pan, toss the tomatoes, eggplant, and garlic cloves with 2 tablespoons of the olive oil, and sprinkle with salt and pepper. Roast for 30 minutes, until the tomatoes begin to caramelize.

While the vegetables are roasting, heat the remaining olive oil in a large soup pot over medium heat. Add the onion and sauté for 3 minutes, until it begins to soften. Add the celery and carrot and sauté for another 3 or 4 minutes, until the onions are translucent. Add the mustard, cumin, coriander, and bay leaf. Mix well.

Add the lentils and the stock or water to the pot, and bring to a boil. Cover and simmer until the lentils are tender, about 20 to 30 minutes. Once the lentils are tender, stir in the tomato-eggplant mixture (scraping the pan well to include all the lovely browned bits). Continue simmering the stew another 20 minutes or so, until the lentils are well done.

Remove the bay leaf. Thin with additional stock or water as desired. Adjust the seasonings with salt and pepper, and perhaps a splash of lemon juice. Finish with an additional drizzle of olive oil.

## INDIAN WOMAN YELLOW BEAN SOUP WITH HARDY GREENS

Indian Woman Yellow beans (also known as Montana Yellow beans) are small and very creamy—a lighter version of black turtle beans. They are an excellent all-purpose heirloom bean: good on their own and equally good in a soup or stew. Another option here would be Hutterite soup beans.

Serves 6 to 8.

**2 cups Indian Woman Yellow beans, sorted and soaked (see page 29)**

**1 Tablespoon olive oil**

**1 large onion, chopped**

**28-ounce can tomatoes or equivalent fresh or frozen**

**2 to 3 cloves garlic, minced**

**3 cups kale or collard greens, center ribs removed and cut into short ribbons**

**2- to 4-inch piece of Parmesan rind**

**2 cups water or broth**

**Salt and pepper to taste**

Drain and rinse the soaked beans and place in a large saucepan. Cover with fresh water by two inches, and bring to a boil. Reduce to a simmer, and cook, partially covered, until the beans are tender but not falling apart, about 45 minutes. Drain and set aside.

While the beans are cooking, heat the olive oil in a heavy soup pot or Dutch oven over medium heat. Add the onions and sauté until translucent. Stir in the tomatoes, garlic, and kale ribbons, and continue cooking until the greens have softened, and the tomatoes have started to break down a bit.

Add the Parmesan rind to the pot along with the beans and the water or broth—you can add more or less liquid depending on how thick you like your soup. Bring the soup back to a simmer and cook for a few minutes, until the flavors have become acquainted. Season to taste with salt and pepper. Remove the Parmesan rind.

Serve garnished with a drizzle of olive oil and a splash of balsamic vinegar, or a sprinkling of grated Parmesan cheese, or a handful of crumbled goat cheese. You could also add a poached egg on top.

**VARIATIONS:** This soup is open to many variations, some of which might include the addition of potatoes, winter squash (try sautéing small cubes of Oregon Sweet Meat and adding them with the greens), chopped carrots, celery or celery root, or other winter root vegetables. If you have leftover wheat berries, rice, or other grains, they would be good, as well. Play with seasonings, too—smoked paprika is yummy, as are toasted and ground cumin seeds. Or try oregano and lots of fresh parsley. A good glug of white wine wouldn't hurt, either. If you want meat, sauté some sausages and add them at the end, or add some shredded leftover roasted chicken.

## NORTH AFRICAN-STYLE GARBANZO BEAN STEW

Garbanzo beans are paired with warm spices, such as turmeric, cinnamon, and cumin, along with winter squash and a garnish of chopped, toasted nuts.

Serves 6 to 8.

**2 Tablespoons olive oil**

**1 small onion, chopped**

**2 cloves garlic, minced**

**1 Tablespoon minced fresh ginger**

**2 pounds winter squash, such as butternut, Oregon Sweet Meat, or Marina di Chiogga, cut into 1-inch cubes**

**4 cups vegetable or chicken stock**

**2 cups cooked garbanzo beans (see page 29)**

**3 medium carrots, peeled and sliced into "pennies"**

**¼ cup currants or raisins**

**2 Tablespoons tomato paste**

**1 teaspoon ground turmeric**

**1 teaspoon ground cinnamon**

**1 teaspoon ground cumin**

**¼ teaspoon chile powder**

**Dash of cayenne pepper**

**Juice from 1 large lime**

**Plain yoghurt**

**Chopped fresh tomato**

**Minced cilantro**

**Chopped, toasted nuts—peanuts, sunflower seeds, almonds**

Heat the oil in a large skillet or soup pot over medium heat. Add the onion and sauté until soft. Add the garlic and ginger, and sauté a few minutes longer. Add the squash and stock, bring to a boil, then reduce the heat and simmer, until the squash is fork tender. Stir in the garbanzo beans, carrots, currants, tomato paste, and spices. Cover and simmer for 20 to 30 minutes, stirring occasionally. When the carrots and squash are very tender, add the lime juice. Season to taste with salt and freshly ground pepper.

Serve in bowls with yoghurt, tomatoes, cilantro, and chopped nuts. Cooked rice and steamed greens under the stew would be good, too.

> **FRESH GINGER**
>
> In the spring, you may find young ginger root in the market. When the skin is thin and tender, you don't have to peel ginger. Most of the time, however, the skin is tougher and should be peeled off. I use a paring knife, but others use a vegetable peeler or a spoon to scrape off the outer skin.
>
> Ginger can be minced by first cutting the root into coins, then into skinny matchsticks, and finally into tiny cubes. If the pieces are not small enough, run your knife through them again to get a fine dice. Alternatively, you can grate ginger using a microplane or a traditional Asian ginger grater. This results in a superfine, almost puréed texture.
>
> Store whole ginger root on the counter for a few days, or longer in a plastic bag in the refrigerator. You can also freeze minced ginger in an airtight container. I've also heard that ginger stores well in a jar of vodka, an intriguing idea that might lend itself well both to future dishes and fancy drinks.

## RIBOLLITA

Ribollita is a Tuscan soup made of beans, day-old bread, and vegetables. Like minestrone (and some say ribollita was traditionally made from leftover minestrone, which makes sense as the word means "reboiled"), there are as many ways to make ribollita as there are beans in the pot. Gather together what you have in the refrigerator, garden, or freezer and proceed from there.

Serves 6 to 8.

**3 Tablespoons olive oil**

**1 onion, chopped**

**3 to 4 stalks celery, chopped**

**2 to 3 carrots, chopped**

**3 medium cloves garlic, chopped**

**2 cups crushed paste tomatoes, or equivalent frozen or canned, with juice reserved**

**¼ to ½ teaspoon crushed red pepper flakes**

**1 pound kale—traditionally Lacinato or dinosaur kale, but any kale will work—center ribs removed and cut into short ribbons**

**½ small green cabbage, shredded—or substitute more kale**

**3 cups cooked white beans—traditionally cannellini, but if you can find them, try white emergo or Borlotti beans (see page 29)**

**4 to 6 cups water or broth**

**4-inch piece of Parmesan rind**

**½ loaf day-old, chewy, whole wheat artisan bread, sourdough bread, or Italian bread**

**1 teaspoon salt or to taste**

**Zest of 1 lemon**

**Grated Parmesan cheese**

**Lemon wedges to pass at the table**

In a large soup pot, heat the olive oil. Add the onion, sauté until softened, then add the celery, carrot, and garlic. Cook for 10 minutes, until the onions are translucent but not browned. Add the tomatoes and their juices and the red pepper flakes, and cook until the tomatoes begin to break down a bit. Stir in the kale, cabbage, beans, water or broth, and the Parmesan rind. Bring to a boil, reduce heat, and simmer until the kale and cabbage are tender, about 15 minutes.

**FINISHING THE SOUP, METHOD I**

Add bite-size chunks of the bread to the soup and simmer, stirring from time to time, until the bread breaks down and the soup thickens, about 20 to 30 minutes. Remove the Parmesan rind, and add the salt, lemon zest, and more liquid if desired.

Serve with a drizzle of fine fruity olive oil, a lemon wedge, and freshly grated Parmesan cheese.

**FINISHING THE SOUP, METHOD II**

After the soup is cooked, remove from the heat and let it cool a bit, or refrigerate and finish your soup the next day. Instead of tearing the bread into bite-size chunks, cut it into six ½-inch thick slices. Line the bottom of a Dutch oven with 2 slices of bread, then add about half the soup. Nestle two more slices of bread on top of that, then add the rest of the soup. Top it off with the remaining 2 slices of bread, and press down to slightly submerge them. Drizzle about ¼ cup of olive oil over the top and sprinkle liberally with grated Parmesan cheese. Bake uncovered at 400°F, for 20 to 25 minutes. Serve as above. This is a particularly gratifying way to finish the soup if you are making it in the depths of winter.

## LEMONY GARBANZO BEAN SOUP

A very bright soup that benefits from a rich flavorful stock and a drizzle of your favorite olive oil at the end. This soup comes together quickly if you have cooked garbanzo beans on hand.

Serves 6 to 8.

**2 cups cooked garbanzo beans (see page 29)**

**2 Tablespoons olive oil, plus extra for the table**

**1 small onion, diced**

**2 cloves garlic, minced**

**1 large or 2 small carrots, finely chopped**

**2 sticks celery, finely chopped**

**1 quart chicken or vegetable stock**

**Juice of one large lemon**

**⅛ to ¼ teaspoon red pepper flakes**

**1 large bay leaf**

**1 cup chopped tomatoes, fresh if in season, frozen or canned if not**

**Grated Parmesan cheese**

**Lemon zest**

**Minced parsley**

**Salt and pepper to taste**

In a large soup pot, heat the olive oil and sauté the onion for a few minutes, then add the garlic and cook until the onion is soft. Add the carrot and celery and sauté a few minutes longer. Now add the stock, lemon juice, red pepper flakes, bay leaf, tomatoes, and garbanzo beans. Simmer until the carrots and celery are tender and the tomatoes are broken down and incorporated into the soup, 10 to 20 minutes, depending on the tomatoes you use. Add salt and pepper to taste.

Serve up the soup and pass olive oil and small bowls of Parmesan cheese, lemon zest, and minced parsley at the table.

# GRAINS

Ask most Americans to describe how they cook with grains, and they probably will tell you about their favorite baked goods, usually involving white flour, perhaps with a bit of whole wheat flour added for its health benefits. When pressed for a list of grains they serve whole, they may mention oats (either made into oatmeal or cookies), rice, or corn, which when popped serves as a handy vehicle for butter.

There is a wide array of whole grains that can be easily incorporated into our day-to-day cooking, providing us with far better nutrition and often presenting far fewer dietary issues, such as gluten intolerance. Some of these grains are becoming more familiar: barley, quinoa, and spelt, for instance. Some are less well known: teff, amaranth, millet, and farro. Actually, amaranth, quinoa, and buckwheat are not true grains, but are grouped with cereal grains because of their nutritional profile and how we prepare them. All grains can be ground into flour, but most are delicious and easy to cook in their whole form (you will hear many whole grains, such as wheat, rye, and oats, called berries or groats, the former being somewhat more pleasing to the ear), and can be incorporated into your meal plan as a substitute for rice. Corn is a bit of the exception to the rule, as the dried kernels need their outer layer (the pericarp) removed before they can be cooked as a whole grain.

**JUST WHAT ARE GRAINS, AND WHEN ARE THEY WHOLE?**

One question that perplexed me for a while is how to define a whole grain. We refer to bread and crackers as being "whole wheat," but are they really composed of whole grains? Is a whole grain one that has not been at all processed or refined? Or is it a grain that has not been ground? One might say that if a grain has all of its parts intact—hull, bran, germ, and endosperm—then it is whole. But really, most grains you purchase are not strictly whole, as the farmer certainly will have processed the grain to the point of removing the stalk and chaff, and probably will have removed the inedible hull as well. Consequently, one might argue that short of wading out into a wheat field and stripping some grains from the stalks, it is not really possible to acquire grain that is completely whole.

Perhaps the question is the level to which the grain has been refined. To my mind, and to the collective minds who make up the Whole Grains Council, a whole grain is one that has not been refined and processed to the point that the bran and the germ have been removed. So brown rice is less refined than white rice. Hulless barley is less refined than pearled barley. Furthermore, whole grains can be purchased intact as berries or groats (least refined), chopped or cut into grits (still technically a whole grain but a bit more refined), steamed and rolled into flakes, or ground into flour (most refined and not whole if the bran and germ have been removed).

In grappling with all this complexity, I find it helpful to remember that grains are seeds, not too far removed from the grass seed you might buy at the hardware store or the weed seeds we toil endlessly to keep out of our gardens. And all grains come equipped with three components wrapped neatly in the hull: the bran, the germ, and the endosperm. The bran and the germ are where the plant stores most of its protein and vitamins, and thus are the most nutritious parts for us to consume (which is why wheat germ is such a popular health food). The endosperm is higher in calories but lower in nutrition. When a grain is refined (think white flour, white rice, and pearled barley), the bran and the germ are removed, and what is left is the less nutritious but oh-so-tasty endosperm.

After a grain has its bran and germ removed, it is much more stable. White flour can sit on your shelf for months and still be edible. Whole grains that have been milled into flour will turn rancid rapidly, unless they are refrigerated or frozen. And refined grains are less appetizing to bugs, which seem to know rather more than we do about what is good for them and are more inclined to go after a grain that is still nutritionally complete.

Because refined grains have such high starch content, starch being the main component of the endosperm, they convert very rapidly to sugar after we eat them. In fact, any grain, refined or otherwise, that has been ground into flour, will convert to sugar faster than a serving of, say, cooked whole wheat berries. Whole grains take longer to digest, which means we feel satisfied longer and don't "crash" as we might after eating a croissant. Like beans, whole grains are high in nutrients and fiber, and also like beans, they are very economical. A slice of store-bought organic whole wheat bread and a quarter cup of cooked wheat berries may have roughly the same caloric value, but the cost of baking, packaging, and shipping the bread will be reflected in the price of the loaf, while the cost of the wheat berries will be but a fraction of that bill.

As with all plants, the ultimate goal of the grain plant is to reproduce—to sprout and to become a new plant. To achieve that goal, all grains contain a substance called phytic acid. Phytic acid helps prevent the seed from being broken down in the digestive tract of animals and therefore enables the grain to survive until it meets with the right environment for growth. This is a great strategy for the plant, but not great for humans who want to eat the grains, as it makes digesting the grain more difficult and prevents us from absorbing the maximum amount of nutrition. If we soak the grains first, as we do beans, not only do they cook faster, they are also easier for our bodies to process.

In many traditional cultures, grains are soaked or sprouted before being eaten. Think sourdough bread or flapjacks, for instance. Oatmeal was traditionally set to soak the night before. And grains are still fermented into a wide variety of beverages, such as the ever-popular beer.

Some people who experience problems with digesting wheat and other grains containing gluten find that they are able to digest soaked or sprouted grains, especially those with lower gluten content. (Other folks simply need to stay away from grains that contain gluten.) Amaranth and buckwheat are said to be gluten-free. Corn, millet, quinoa, rice, and teff all have very low gluten content. Spelt,

Kamut, and farro (or emmer) are older strains of wheat that are lower in gluten than newer strains. Barley, rye, and oats also have less gluten than conventional wheat. And when the grain is sprouted, some of the gluten will be "used up" by the embryonic plant, thus increasing the cereal's digestibility for those who are somewhat sensitive to this substance.

**ABOUT THE RECIPES**

Whole grains are delicious simply cooked in water or broth and served as a substitute for rice, or enhanced with flavorings and vegetables as you would a pilaf. Whole grains are also wonderful in salads, as an addition to soups (think chicken soup with rice), or served up as a bowl of porridge for breakfast. Since many people are not familiar with the many ways whole grains can be incorporated into the diet, the majority of the recipes in this section explore cooking with wheat berries, rye berries, barley, and other grains. While most recipes feature grain berries, others call for grains that have been steamed and rolled or cut (such as bulgur wheat and oatmeal), ground coarsely (as in the case of polenta), or milled into flour (but a true whole grain flour), simply because these ingredients are so easy find and cook with and also, let's face it, because they are so delicious!

**COOKING WITH WHOLE GRAINS**

Most grains are very easy going and don't require a great deal of fussing. It is a good idea to rinse and sort your grains to make sure there are no bits of stem or chaff left behind. As with beans, many grains benefit from a good soak but can be cooked just as well without. And as with beans, if you can, cook more than you need and freeze the rest or use it later in the week. The leftover grains from today's cooking can be made into a salad tomorrow, or added to a soup or stew, or folded into a frittata. Or the next morning, add leftover grains to a pot with some milk, and simmer them until you have a quick porridge.

Once you become comfortable with the basics of cooking whole grains, you may want to take it a step further. Check out the recipes for risotto and pilaf, and start experimenting with adding spices, herbs, and other vegetables to your grains. Try some meals featuring grains as the main course. And don't forget about dessert! Whole grain puddings can satisfy the sweet tooth but still contribute to your and your family's health.

## AN OVERVIEW OF GRAINS

Following is a brief introduction to the grains presently available in the Pacific Northwest. A few are not being farmed commercially at present, but hopefully they will be more widely grown here in the future.

### THE BIG BERRIES

**Wheat Berries, Farro, Emmer, Spelt, and Kamut** are all forms of wheat and as such, all behave in much the same manner. You may also see these grains rolled into flakes like oatmeal, and indeed they can be cooked like oatmeal for your morning porridge.

Farro or emmer, actually two names for the same grain, is a staple in Italy. Hard red wheat (also called hard winter wheat) berries are very dense and chewy, while soft white wheat berries (also called spring wheat) are somewhat more delicate in texture and flavor. Spelt is bigger than either hard or soft wheat, has more protein than modern wheat strains, and is sweet and nutty tasting. Kamut is even larger and is wonderfully buttery and chewy.

**Barley.** Most barley recipes in this book call for golden or purple hulless barley (also called Purple Karma barley). If you can't find those, substitute hulled barley, or as a last resort, pearled barley. The latter will not have quite the nutritional value of hulless barley, but it will cook a bit faster and will be delicious nonetheless. Barley releases a lot of starch as it cooks, resulting in a creamy texture, and is thus very amenable to use in soup, stew, risotto, and porridge.

**Oats.** Oat berries (also called oat groats) are oat grains that have been hulled but are not otherwise processed. Steel-cut oats contain more nutrients than rolled oats, as they have undergone less processing. Rolled oats, either the thick "old-fashioned" type or the so-called "instant" or quick oats, have been steamed and then rolled. Instant or quick oats are simply rolled oats that have been cut into smaller pieces to make them cook faster. Steel-cut oats take a bit longer to cook into porridge and have a chewier texture and a nuttier flavor than rolled oats. But rolled oats are still considered to be a whole grain, as they have not had the bran removed, just the inedible outer hull. Oat berries make a lovely pilaf when sautéed with onions, then cooked with dried cranberries or currants and garnished with toasted nuts. They are also wonderful in savory side dishes and salads.

**Rye.** Most of us are familiar with rye bread, which is usually flavored with caraway seeds. Caraway is objectionable to some people, and as a result, they believe they do not like rye. On its own, rye is tangy and nutty and not at all strong flavored. Rye berries are very chewy and dense, even when fully cooked, and make a wonderful base for a grain salad. Rye is also rolled into flakes.

# BASIC BIG BERRY GRAIN COOKING

**SORT**

Before you cook the big berries, you first want to sort them as you do beans, removing any bits of chaff or earth or small pebbles that may have found their way into the bag. Pick out any grains that still have their husk attached. I find spreading the grains out on a baking sheet works well for this step.

**SOAK**

Next, put your grains in a large bowl and fill it with water. Any grains that escaped the de-husking process and your sharp eyes will float to the top. Skim them off and discard. Rinse the grains several times, until the water runs clear.

Soak the grains as you would beans: in a large bowl, with water to cover by an inch or so, either overnight or all day while you are out and about. If you don't have time to soak your grains, don't fret. Just plan on a slightly longer cooking time.

**SEASON**

Rather than salting the cooking water, I generally add salt after the grains have cooked. However, for a delicate flavoring, herbs, spices, and other aromatics can be added to grains while they cook. Try adding a few cardamom pods and a cinnamon stick, for instance, or a sprig of rosemary or thyme and a bay leaf. Barley benefits from being cooked with a strip of lemon peel and peppercorns.

**SIMMER**

When you are ready to cook, place your grains in a large pot with a tight-fitting lid and add water—roughly three times the water as the amount of grains. Bring the water to a boil, reduce to a simmer, cover, and cook until the grains are tender. It is fine to peek inside and see how the grains are coming along. If the grains are done and there is still liquid left in the pot, simply drain it off. If all the water has been absorbed and the grain is not as done as you would like, add more (best to use warm water or broth) and cook a bit longer. When soaked, most of the big berries will take about 30 to 45 minutes to cook. Barley takes a bit longer, 45 minutes to an hour.

Remember that fresh grains—those that have been recently harvested—will cook faster and require less liquid than grains that are over a year old. When cooking grains, it is best to avoid stirring until they are done. As to when they are done—what do you like? Some people like their rice and wheat berries and barley cooked until very soft. Some like them with a bit more bite. It's up to you!

### THE SMALL SEEDY CHARACTERS

Though they are technically seeds, since we use them as grains, these small seeds are included here. They do not need or want to be soaked and take very well to being toasted before they are cooked.

**Amaranth** is the very tiny seed of a plant in the goosefoot family, which makes it a relative of chard and spinach. It contains a complete protein, along with ample amounts of calcium and iron. It was an important crop in the pre-colonial Americas and was used by the Aztecs in religious ceremonies. Amaranth is often described as having an earthy or grassy flavor. When cooked, the seeds release a lot of starch, making it an excellent addition to porridge.

To cook, combine 1 cup of amaranth with 2½ cups of water and bring to a boil. Cover and simmer for 15 to 20 minutes. Let sit for 5 to 10 minutes before fluffing. Dress up your amaranth a bit with fresh herbs, a squeeze of lemon juice, and some olive oil.

**Millet** has, in the U.S. anyway, the unfortunate reputation of being birdseed. In many other countries, it is still eaten daily, by humans. There are many different types of millet, and at one point in time, various millets were grown throughout Italy and north into Austria, Switzerland, and Romania, and south into India and Africa. In most of those places, corn has replaced millet as the grain of choice for porridge and bread, but millet is still an important staple in India and Africa.

Millet is gluten-free and very high in antioxidants and magnesium.

Millet can be cooked toasted or untoasted. Toasting the grains before cooking makes them fluffier and drier, while cooking untoasted millet results in a stickier texture.

**TOASTED:** Heat 2 teaspoons of butter or oil in a large saucepan and add 1 cup of millet. Stir constantly over medium heat for 2 to 3 minutes, until the millet smells nutty and starts to pop. Or toast in a dry cast-iron skillet and then transfer to the cooking pot. Add 2 cups of boiling water, stir, and return to a boil. Reduce to a simmer, and cook, covered, over very low heat for 18 to 20 minutes, then let stand another 10 minutes.

**UNTOASTED:** Bring 2 cups of water to a boil in a large saucepan and slowly add 1 cup of millet. Return to a boil, reduce to a simmer, and cook, covered, for 18 to 20 minutes. Let stand another 10 minutes.

For a porridge-like texture, increase the amount of cooking liquid to 3 cups, some of which can be milk (dairy or otherwise).

**Quinoa** is native to the arid mountains and coastal valleys of Peru, Ecuador, Chile, and Bolivia. Like millet, amaranth, and teff, it is a seed (related to beets and spinach and thus amaranth), and high in calcium, phosphorus, and iron as well as being gluten-free. Over the last few years, its popularity has increased in the U.S., but until quite recently all quinoa has been imported. Now, however, Washington State University is working on developing varieties suited to North America, and small-scale farmers in the Pacific Northwest are experimenting with growing quinoa.

Before cooking, thoroughly rinse 1 cup of quinoa by covering it with cold water in a bowl and then draining it through a strainer. Allow the grains to dry for about 20 minutes. Place the quinoa in a 2-quart saucepan, and toast it for about 5 minutes, stirring constantly. When the quinoa smells nutty, add 1½ cups of boiling water or stock. Lower the heat, cover, and simmer the quinoa, for 10 to 12 minutes, until all the water is absorbed and you see the little curlicues emerge. Allow to rest for 5 minutes, then fluff with a fork.

**Teff** is reputed to have originated in Ethiopia about 4000 to 1000 B.C.E. It leads other grains—by a wide margin—in its calcium content, and is also an excellent source of vitamin C, a nutrient not commonly found in grains. It is high in resistant starch, a type of fiber that is helpful in managing blood sugar levels and controlling weight, and it is gluten-free.

Since teff's bran and germ make up such a large percentage of the tiny grain, teff has traditionally been eaten in its whole form. It is now also available ground into flour.

Whole grain teff can be cooked untoasted or toasted. Toasting the grain before cooking gives it a mellow, somewhat sweet taste and a crunchy texture.

**TOASTED:** In a large saucepan, heat 2 tablespoons of butter or olive oil and stir in 1 cup of teff grain. Cook over medium heat, stirring constantly, until the grains release a pleasant fragrance. Or toast in a dry cast-iron skillet and then transfer to the cooking pot. Add 1½ cups of boiling water (carefully, as it will sputter a bit), bring back to a boil, and cover. Simmer over very low heat for 15 minutes, or until done to taste. Increase the amount of water to 2½ cups for a more porridge-like texture.

**UNTOASTED:** In a large saucepan, bring 3 cups of water to a boil and slowly add the teff grain, stirring constantly. Bring the mixture back to a boil, then simmer, covered, for 15 minutes, or until done to taste.

### AND A FEW OTHER GRAINS

**Buckwheat** is yet another pseudo-grain, the seed of a plant related to rhubarb. It is sold in several forms. Whole unhulled buckwheat is dark in color and is wonderful when ground into flour for incorporating into buckwheat pancakes or other baked goods. Whole hulled buckwheat can be cooked into a pilaf or similar grain dish. Whole hulled buckwheat is also available toasted, in which case it is often referred to as kasha.

**Corn** is one of those plants that straddles two categories. Fresh corn is classified as a vegetable, but dried corn is referred to as a grain. And, as with other grains, it offers an array of nutrients—in particular, vitamin A, more than ten times that of other grains. Corn is also high in antioxidants and the carotenoids that are associated with eye health. A gluten-free grain, corn can be a staple ingredient for those who are gluten intolerant.

In many traditional cultures, corn is eaten with beans, as the two have complementary amino acids that work together to provide a complete protein. In Central and South America, and in many parts of the U.S., corn is often nixtamalized—soaked in an alkaline solution (often lime-water)—then drained and made into flour. The nixtamalization process makes many of the corn kernels' B vitamins more available to us and also adds some calcium. Even though a small amount of bran is lost in the soaking process, nixtamalized corn is still considered a whole grain. Hominy is made of nixtamalized corn, and tortillas and tamales are made of nixtamalized corn that has been ground and mixed into a dough called masa.

Several types of corn are used as grain, and they are differentiated by the amount of hard versus soft starch in the corn kernels. Flint corn contains the highest amount of hard starch, and is the kind of corn typically used for polenta and hominy. Dent corn has some hard starch but more soft starch, and is good for tortillas and cornbread. Flour corn is the highest in soft starch and, as you might guess from the name, is best suited for grinding into a fine flour. Popcorn has a soft starch interior surrounded by a hard starch exterior, and when heated the inside explodes into the form we all love to munch.

Whether you are enjoying ground corn or want to try making your own hominy, you will probably notice that the locally grown varieties of dried corn, such as Abenaki Flint, Roy's Calais Flint, and Amish Butter, are as wildly different from the generic Midwestern corn as the heirloom beans are from canned beans. The world of corn is so complex and intriguing that it merits its own book— I urge you to read Anthony Boutard's recent treatise, *Beautiful Corn*.

**Bulgur Wheat.** I debated for quite a while over where to include bulgur wheat. It is not a unique grain, but a form of wheat that has been parboiled and then cracked. But it is not a wheat berry, either. Whole wheat bulgur is, like rolled oats, a whole grain that has been refined to make it easier to cook. It is wonderful to have on hand because it is so easy and fast to prepare. There are two methods:

**COARSELY GROUND BULGUR:** Bring 2 cups of water or stock to boil in a pot. Add 1 cup of bulgur and any seasonings you might like. Cover and reduce to a simmer. Cook for 20 minutes, then remove from heat, and let rest for another 10 minutes. Fluff with a fork.

**FINELY GROUND BULGUR:** Bring the same ratio (2 to 1) of water to a boil, and simply pour the water over the bulgur in a bowl. Cover and let sit 20 to 30 minutes, until all the water has been absorbed. The bulgur should be somewhat chewy but not hard.

**Wild Rice** and domestic rice are not the same plant. And like buckwheat and quinoa, wild rice is not really a cereal grain but is treated like one. It is one of the few cereals indigenous to North America. Wild rice is still gathered by hand from canoes on lakes in Minnesota and Wisconsin, but it is also now cultivated in Oregon. It contains large amounts of protein, minerals, B vitamins, folic acid, and carbohydrates. Cooked wild rice has a rich, nutty flavor, sometimes described as smoky, and a wonderfully chewy texture.

Like many other grains, wild rice is great as a breakfast cereal. The easiest way to enjoy it in the morning is to cook a little extra for dinner. Put the leftover wild rice into a saucepan with 2 or 3 tablespoons of water to moisten. Cover the pot, and warm briefly over medium heat. Enjoy in a bowl with some soy milk or nut milk, a sprinkling of cinnamon, and a touch of maple syrup.

Cooked wild rice also makes a great salad when mixed with fresh vegetables such as cucumbers, celery, tomatoes, scallions, bell peppers, carrots, and cabbage. Add a few chopped raw nuts and season with a hint of fresh minced sage and oregano, lemon juice, a little rice, balsamic or raspberry vinegar, salt, and pepper. Or add some wild rice to soup.

To cook, sort and rinse 1 cup of wild rice. Add it to a pot with 3 cups of boiling water. Return to a boil and stir. Reduce heat and simmer, covered, 50 to 60 minutes, until the kernels just puff open. Uncover and fluff with a fork. Simmer for 5 additional minutes. Drain any excess liquid. For a chewier texture, decrease the cooking time.

## SPROUTING GRAINS

Sprouting your grain yields several benefits. The sprouting process increases the vitamin content; it neutralizes the phytic acid to a further extent than soaking does, making the minerals in the grain more available; and it makes the grain even easier to digest. Although it takes a few days to sprout grains, it's not overly labor-intensive. The berries (wheat, rye, spelt, Kamut, and farro) can all be sprouted using the same basic instructions, though the germination time may vary somewhat. Corn, buckwheat, and the smaller seeds are not good candidates for sprouting.

Start with clean, organic, untreated grain. Sort through the grains to make sure all pebbles, chaff, and hulls are removed, and rinse thoroughly.

Place the grain in a ceramic or stainless-steel crock or a glass mason jar. Add warm water to about an inch above the level of the grain, and soak overnight.

In the morning, drain and rinse well. Throughout the day, rinse multiple times, then drain well.

Continue rinsing the grain for two to three days, until the grains have sprouted to your liking. Most people stop when the tail is as long as the grain itself. Don't let them go so long that leaves form.

Rinse the sprouted grains one last time, drain, and either refrigerate them or dehydrate them to grind into flour. Sprouted grains are great for salads or as an addition to breads.

# GRAINS FOR BREAKFAST

Breakfast may be the first meal you think of when you ponder how to incorporate more whole grains into your diet. Whole grains are a great way to start the day, and there are a lot of ways to make it easy to cook them, even on Thursday morning when you have an eight o'clock meeting and three kids to get off to school.

Leftover grains transform themselves into whole grain breakfasts in a snap. Consider:

**Breakfast Burrito.** Scramble an egg, heat up some leftover grains such as brown rice, grate a bit of cheese, chop a tomato, and fold it all together in a warm flour tortilla, burrito style. Or fold the tortilla in half and grill it for a breakfast quesadilla.

**Grilled Polenta or Teffolenta.** Slice up some leftover Polenta (page 131) or Teffolenta (page 134) and cook over medium heat on a greased griddle, until golden brown and warmed through. Serve as you would French toast, with butter and a drizzle of maple syrup, or top it with a fried or poached egg.

**Breakfast Bowl.** Leftover rice, quinoa, barley, or whatever other grains you have cooked up the night before or on the weekend, make a wonderful morning bowl. Place a scoop of cooked grain in a pot with about 1½ times as much milk or soy milk or water as you have grains. Add a sprinkling of cinnamon to the milk or water, and toss in some dried fruit, frozen berries, or finely chopped fresh apple. Bring to a boil, reduce to a simmer, and cook until the grain is soft, about 10 to 15 minutes, depending on the grain. Top with maple syrup or honey and perhaps some toasted nuts.

Whole grains are also found in other traditional morning menu items. Pancakes, muffins, and of course hot cereal can all be made with whole grains, and though they are a bit more time consuming, many can be made ahead of time.

**PORRIDGE POSSIBILITIES**

I am very fond of the word porridge. It has such a comforting sound, and when I say "I am making porridge for breakfast," I have the sense that everyone is going to go off into the world with a full belly and a warm glow about them. But you can call it hot cereal, too, and if you are making hot cereal with oats you can call it oatmeal. Whatever you call it, porridge is a great way to start your day. Porridge also is a wonderful way to economize, because making your own is vastly less expensive than buying a box of processed cereal. And, of course, it is far more nutritious.

Do you know how to make oatmeal? I mean the kind your grandmother made, not the stuff you zap in the microwave. It's really not hard nor does it take a long time.

**OATMEAL**

Serves 4.

**1 cup rolled oats—old-fashioned or thick-rolled, not instant**

**2 to 2½ cups milk or water, or half milk and half water**

**Chopped dried fruit, stick of cinnamon, nut butter (optional)**

In a pot, combine the oats and liquid. The less liquid you use, the thicker your oatmeal will be. Add a pinch of salt if you like. Bring to a boil, turn down to simmer, and let cook for about 10 minutes, until the oatmeal reaches the consistency you prefer. Stir occasionally, especially if you are using milk. If you prefer chewier, less creamy oatmeal, bring the liquid to a boil first, then add the oats and cover the pot. You can toss in some dried fruit or a stick of cinnamon while it is cooking to jazz things up. Top your oatmeal with milk or cream or yoghurt and whatever sweetener your heart desires, and you have one good meal under your belt. Some folks even stir in a bit of almond or peanut butter.

Oatmeal can also be made with steel-cut oats, sometimes referred to as Scottish oats. They take a bit longer to cook as they have not been steamed as rolled oats have. Soaking steel-cut oats overnight reduces the cooking time. Combine 1 cup of steel-cut oats with 4 parts water, and let it sit overnight in the cooking pot. In the morning, add a pinch of salt, bring to a boil, reduce to a simmer, and cook for about 10 to 15 minutes, until it reaches your preferred consistency. Alternatively, if you are stricken with the urge to make porridge with steel-cut oats in the morning and haven't put it up to soak, simply bring the water to a boil in your porridge pot, add a pinch of salt and the oats, and reduce to a simmer. Cover the pot, and cook for about 30 minutes, depending on how toothsome you like your cereal.

### PORRIDGE AND SPURTLES

My grandmother didn't have one, but I do. Back in the fifteenth century, when a great many people made porridge on a regular basis, the Scots developed the spurtle. Originally a flat, spatula-like utensil used for flipping oatcakes, over time the tool became a fat wooden dowel, often with a contoured end to provide a better grip. It was (and is) used for stirring porridge and preventing it from congealing and becoming lumpy. The spurtle gained such importance in Scottish porridge making that, at the World Porridge-Making Championship held each year in Carrbridge, Inverness-shire, in Scotland, the prize for the best bowl of porridge is a golden spurtle. You can get a spurtle, too, from Bob's Red Mill in Portland or from Tim Cebulla of Medford, Oregon, who makes spurtles out of Oregon myrtlewood.

## CROCKPOT GRAIN PARTY PORRIDGE

Perhaps you have a full house, and they are all going to want breakfast in the morning, and maybe you are not so much into cooking breakfast or at least not for so very many people. Or maybe you have a few kids in school, all of whom need a good bowl of hot cereal in them before they go out the door, but you are daunted by the idea of cooking porridge every morning. Grain party!

**2 cups brown rice**

**1 cup rolled oats**

**½ cup steel-cut oats**

**1 cup wheat berries**

**½ cup hulless barley, sorted and soaked (see page 111)**

**7 to 8 cups water — more water the longer you sleep**

**½ Tablespoon cinnamon or 1 small stick**

**1 teaspoon vanilla**

**¼ teaspoon salt**

**1 cup dried fruit (optional)**

Combine all the ingredients in a crockpot or slow cooker. Set it on low just before you go to bed, and turn it off as soon as you wake up. Serve with whatever toppings you are inclined to decorate with, and dig in. It is as simple as that.

You can also add quinoa, amaranth, millet, or whatever other grains you have on hand. Just keep the proportion of 1 to 2½ or 3, depending on how thick you like your cereal and how long you like (or are allowed) to sleep. Refrigerate any leftovers and heat them up with milk the next morning.

## TOASTED BULGUR WHEAT PORRIDGE WITH APPLES

Serves 3 to 4.

**1 cup diced fresh apple**

**2 Tablespoons butter**

**1 cup bulgur wheat**

**3 cups water**

**½ teaspoon ground cinnamon**

**¼ teaspoon ground cardamom**

Melt the butter in a 3-quart saucepan, and add the diced apple and the spices. Sauté over medium heat for a few minutes, until the apple begins to soften. Now add the bulgur wheat and stir to coat. Toast over medium heat for 3 to 4 minutes, stirring often.

Bring the water to a boil, then carefully add it to the wheat and apples. Lower the heat, cover, and simmer until all the water has been absorbed, about 15 minutes. Serve with honey and milk.

**VARIATION:** You can also make this porridge with dried apples. Soak the apples in a bowl of hot water, until soft, then chop, and add them to the toasted bulgur wheat when you add the water. For a bigger apple hit, try cooking the wheat in apple cider, or top each serving with a spoonful of apple butter.

## TEFF, FLAX & OATMEAL PORRIDGE

Contributed by Karen Guillemin.

This has become one of our family's favorite hot cereal combinations. Serves 3 to 4.

**¾ cups oats**

**⅛ cup teff grain**

**⅛ cup flax seeds**

**1 Tablespoon butter**

**Boiling water**

The evening before, set a kettle of water to boil. In a saucepan, melt the butter and add the oats, teff, and flax seeds. Cook, stirring, for about 5 minutes, until the grains are toasted and very fragrant. Turn off the heat. Carefully add ⅔ cups of boiling water (it will splatter), stir, and cover.

The next morning, add ⅓ cup of boiling water to the pan and reheat (for a richer porridge, use ⅓ cup milk). Let the oatmeal and teff mixture simmer for about 5 to 8 minutes, until it is the desired tenderness and thickness. Serve warm, sprinkled with your preferred toppings and a splash of cold milk.

**VARIATION:** You can, of course, cook this all at once if you have time in the morning. Simply add 3 cups of boiling water to the toasted grains and cook for about 15 minutes.

## PANCAKES

Sunday morning pancakes—a long-standing tradition in our family. Should there be any pancakes leftover, they can be refrigerated and popped into the toaster oven on Monday morning. Or save some batter, in a covered container in the refrigerator, and cook up a few fresh cakes.

### BASIC WHOLE GRAIN PANCAKES

Makes 4 to 8 pancakes.

**1½ cups whole wheat flour**

**½ cup rye flour**

**½ teaspoon salt**

**2 Tablespoons sugar**

**1 Tablespoon baking powder**

**3 eggs, beaten**

**⅓ cup melted butter or oil, plus extra for cooking**

**2 cups buttermilk, or 1½ cups milk plus ½ cup plain yoghurt**

Mix the dry ingredients together in a large bowl. Mix the wet ingredients together in a small bowl. Add the wet mix to the dry, stirring only until the dry mix is moistened.

Heat a cast-iron griddle over medium heat, and grease it with a swirl of oil or a bit of butter. When the griddle is hot enough for water droplets to dance, ladle on about ½ cup of the batter. Cook until bubbles appear on the surface and the edges look firm, then flip and cook on the other side.

**VARIATIONS:** Decrease the whole wheat flour to 1 cup and add ½ cup of stone-ground cornmeal, or ¼ cup of cornmeal and ¼ cup of buckwheat. Play around with different grain combinations until you find the one you like best, or vary according to what you have in your pantry.

## CHIA SEED AND BUCKWHEAT PANCAKES

Contributed by Karen Guillemin.

Makes about 32 pancakes.

**¼ cup chia seeds**

**2 cups buttermilk**

**2 eggs, beaten**

**3 Tablespoons canola oil**

**½ cup buckwheat flour**

**½ cup white flour**

**1 teaspoon baking powder**

**¼ teaspoon baking soda**

**Pinch of salt**

**Butter or oil for cooking**

In a large mixing bowl, combine the chia seeds with the buttermilk. If you'd like the chia seeds to be very soft, you can soak them in the buttermilk overnight, but they will soften up quite nicely in about 10 minutes while you start the batter. Mix in the eggs and canola oil.

In a separate bowl, mix together the remaining dry ingredients. Then, gently mix the dry ingredients into the wet ingredients until they are just combined.

Heat a griddle or large skillet over medium heat. Melt a small bit of butter or oil to grease the surface. Spoon on dollops of batter with a soup spoon and allow to cook until the batter loses some of its raw pale color and bubbles stay fixed. Flip and cook for a minute on the other side. Both sides should be nicely browned. Transfer to a warm plate. Enjoy with fruit toppings and maple syrup.

## TEFF AND RICOTTA PANCAKES WITH APPLE TOPPING

Contributed by Karen Guillemin.

Light and delicate with a slight pop from the teff.

Makes 6 to 10 pancakes.

**¼ cup teff grain**

**1 cup water**

**Pinch of salt**

**½ cup ricotta cheese**

**2 eggs, separated**

**¾ cup buttermilk**

**½ cup flour—unbleached all-purpose or whole wheat pastry flour, or substitute other flours, or use teff flour to makes these gluten-free**

**1 teaspoon baking powder**

**½ teaspoon baking soda**

**1 Tablespoon brown sugar**

**Butter or oil for cooking**

Cook the teff in the cup of water with a pinch of salt, simmering for about 20 minutes and stirring occasionally, until the water is absorbed.

Mix together the ricotta, egg yolks, buttermilk, and cooked teff. In another bowl, combine the flour, baking powder, baking soda, and brown sugar. In a third bowl, beat the egg whites until stiff.

Mix the dry ingredients into the ricotta mixture, until they are just incorporated. Then, gently fold the egg whites into the batter.

Heat a griddle, and when it is warm, grease with a little butter or oil. Use a soup spoon to spoon on the batter. When permanent bubbles form and the color of the batter lightens, flip the pancakes and cook them for a couple more minutes. Serve the pancakes hot off the griddle with the Apple Topping and a bit of maple syrup.

## APPLE TOPPING

**2 apples, cored and chopped into ½-inch pieces**

**2 Tablespoons butter**

**½ teaspoon cinnamon**

**1 teaspoon sugar**

Warm a small skillet over medium-low heat. Melt the butter, and stir in the chopped apples and cinnamon. Cook over low heat for about 15 minutes, stirring occasionally, until the apples are soft and fragrant. Stir in the sugar, cook for a minute longer and set aside.

## MORE PANCAKE TOPPING IDEAS

Pancakes topped with maple syrup are pretty hard to beat, but there are other possibilities to consider. Try topping your stack of cakes with your favorite jam or fruit conserve, such as lingonberries. Sauté pear slices in butter and sugar with a dash of cinnamon, and slather that concoction over your pancakes. Or make some quick berry syrup: In a small saucepan, combine a cup or so of berries (blueberries, blackberries, raspberries, or whatever berries are at hand) with ¼ to ½ cup of sugar (depending on how sweet you like your syrup and how tangy your berries are), and perhaps a bit of lemon peel, a dash of vanilla, or other spices. Add a splash of water and bring to a simmer. Cook over low heat, for 10 to 15 minutes, until the berries soften and start to dissolve. You can add a bit more water if needed. When the berries have cooked down to your liking, serve directly or mash them a bit and strain if there are a great many seeds.

## OVERNIGHT OATMEAL-SESAME PANCAKES

Makes 4 to 6 pancakes.

**2 cups regular rolled oats or steel-cut oats**

**½ cup boiling water (if using steel-cut oats)**

**2 cups buttermilk, or 1½ cups milk plus ½ cup yoghurt**

**2 eggs, beaten**

**2 Tablespoons melted butter**

**½ cup whole wheat flour**

**2 Tablespoons sugar**

**1 teaspoon baking soda**

**¼ cup sesame seeds**

**Butter or oil for cooking**

If you are using steel-cut oats, pour ½ cup of boiling water over them and mix well. Heat the buttermilk or milk/yoghurt mix and stir into the oats. For rolled oats, omit the boiling water and simply combine with the warmed buttermilk. Soak the batter overnight in a bowl covered with a tea towel.

In the morning, stir the eggs and melted butter into the oat mixture. In a separate bowl, combine the flour, sugar, and baking soda, then add to the wet mix. Stir until well combined. This will probably make a thicker pancake batter than what you are used to. If it is too stiff, add a splash of milk.

Heat a skillet and add a bit of butter or a swirl of oil. Add pancake batter by the ladleful and sprinkle about ½ teaspoon of sesame seeds over the surface. Cook over medium-low heat, until bubbles break on the surface and the pancakes look firm around the edges. Flip and cook until the other side is golden brown. These pancakes need a bit more cooking time than average pancakes, so keep the heat on the low side.

As with many things in life, these are excellent when adorned with a bit of butter and whatever pancake embellishments you favor.

## CORNMEAL PANCAKES

Katherine Deumling of Cook With What You Have contributed this recipe, inspired by the *Joy of Cooking*. She says these are her family's favorite pancakes. They are thin, delicate, and fragrant.

Makes 6 to 8 pancakes.

**1 cup medium or coarse cornmeal — Katherine always uses Ayers Creek cornmeal, either Amish Butter or Roy's Calais**

**1 teaspoon salt**

**1 Tablespoon honey**

**1 cup boiling water**

**1 large egg**

**½ cup whole milk**

**2 Tablespoons melted butter**

**½ cup plus 1 Tablespoon whole wheat flour or all-purpose flour**

**2 teaspoons baking powder**

**Zest of one lemon, finely grated**

**Butter or oil for cooking**

In a medium bowl, whisk the salt into the cornmeal. Carefully whisk in the boiling water and honey. Cover the bowl with a plate or lid, and let stand for 10 minutes.

Meanwhile, in another bowl, whisk the egg with the milk and melted butter. In a third bowl, combine the flour and baking powder. With a few quick strokes, whisk the egg and milk mixture into the cornmeal, then add the lemon zest and flour. Stir until just combined. The batter will be fairly thin.

Coat the bottom of a heavy skillet with butter or oil and heat until hot but not smoking. Spoon on about 2 to 3 tablespoons of batter per pancake. Flip as soon as the edges turn golden and bubbles begin forming on the top. They cook quickly!

# MAINS WITH GRAINS

There are many ways to work whole grains into main dishes. The following recipes cast grains in the leading role rather than relegating them to the supporting cast. Some of these recipes call for meat, others don't, although the latter would certainly accommodate the addition of meat in whatever form you prefer.

**POLENTA**

Polenta is the Italian term for cornmeal mush. Some people are very fond of cornmeal mush for breakfast. My grandfather was one, and he always ate it with honey, butter, and heavy cream (not being inclined to limit himself to only one form of dairy fat in any given meal). You can eat cornmeal mush for dinner, too, but it sounds much more sophisticated if you call it polenta.

Whatever you call it, polenta is made from coarsely ground corn, water, and a bit of salt. You can substitute milk or stock for part or all of the water, and you can add butter or cheese (or both) at the end. You can add minced dried tomatoes or spices. You get the idea. It's flexible stuff!

Any number of *nonnas* (Italian grandmothers) will tell you that you must stir your polenta constantly while it is cooking, and that moreover, you must stir always in the same direction. This is to keep the polenta at an even boil, to prevent lumps from forming, and to keep the bottom from scorching. In my experience, constant stirring for the first ten minutes or so is really important (and I must confess I always stir in the same direction). After the polenta has thickened, I find that if I keep the heat low and cover the pot, I can turn my back on it and do other things, as long as I turn back and give it a stir fairly often. However, if you have a child or a spouse (or a sous chef) at hand who is in need of employment, by all means hand them the spoon and tell them to stir, constantly, and always in the same direction.

The polenta is done when it is very thick, starts to resist being stirred a bit, and pulls away from the side of the pot when you pass a spoon through it. You can also taste a bit of it to be sure the corn particles are tender—no one wants gritty polenta.

Once cooked, polenta can be spooned into a bowl and eaten plain, or topped with your favorite tomato sauce and perhaps some grilled sweet Italian sausage. It can also be poured onto a greased baking sheet, spread smooth, and cooled. When cool, polenta is firm enough to cut into squares which can be grilled or fried—polenta crostini! Top the grilled squares with a dab of pesto or broil some cheese on top, and you have yourself an excellent appetizer. Alternatively, use the slabs of polenta to make baked polenta lasagna, as in Polenta Pasticciata (page 132).

### BASIC POLENTA

**2 cups coarse cornmeal—also known as polenta—especially tasty and increasingly available at farmers markets is Abenaki Flint (also called Roy's Calais Flint) and other types of flint corn polenta**

**7 cups water**

**Scant ½ Tablespoon salt**

In a large saucepan, combine the water and salt, and bring to a boil. Stirring constantly with a whisk, slowly pour in the cornmeal. Reduce the heat to medium and continue to stir without interruption. After about 10 minutes, when the polenta has started to thicken, you can turn the heat down to low, cover the pot, and move on to other activities in the kitchen, but do give it a stir every so often. Depending on the corn you are using, it can take 30 to 45 minutes for the polenta to fully cook.

## POLENTA PASTICCIATA DI MAMA ELIN
### (Baked Polenta in the Style of Mama Elin)

Serves 6 to 8.

*Pasticciata* (pronounced pah-stee-*chyah*-tah) means "messed up" in Italian. Polenta crostini are layered with a rich tomato sauce and grated cheese in the manner of lasagna.

### THE POLENTA CROSTINI

Prepare one recipe of Basic Polenta (page 131).

Pour the polenta onto a lightly greased baking sheet, and spread it out evenly with a spatula dipped in water. Let it set for about 20 minutes (or make ahead of time and keep it covered in the refrigerator). Cut into 2-inch squares.

### THE TOMATO SAUCE

¼ to ½ cup dried porcini mushrooms

4 Tablespoons olive oil

1 small onion, finely chopped

1 large carrot, minced

2 stalks celery, minced

¼ cup flat leaf parsley, minced

2 Tablespoons tomato paste

½ cup red wine

2½ cups canned tomatoes, chopped, with juice reserved

Salt and pepper to taste

¼ pound <u>each</u>: fontina and provolone cheese, grated

Grated Parmesan cheese for the top

Preheat the oven to 450°F.

Soak the dried mushrooms in hot water until very soft, about 20 to 30 minutes. Drain, reserving the liquid. Chop coarsely.

Heat the olive oil in a saucepan, and add the onion, carrot, celery, and parsley. Sauté gently until softened, about 10 minutes.

Add the mushrooms, reserved mushroom liquid, tomato paste, and wine. Simmer for a few minutes, then add the tomatoes and their juice. Season to taste with salt and pepper, and simmer, stirring occasionally, for about 30 minutes, until the sauce has thickened somewhat.

**ASSEMBLE THE DISH:** Lightly grease a 9 x 13-inch glass pan. Arrange the polenta squares in the pan, and cover with a layer of sauce and a scattering of fontina and provolone cheese. Repeat, alternating layers of polenta, sauce, and cheese, finishing with cheese on the top. You don't need to drench the polenta with sauce, a thin layer is fine. There may be sauce left over. Scatter some grated Parmesan cheese over the surface.

Bake 15 to 20 minutes, until the casserole is bubbling and the cheese is golden. Let rest for 15 minutes before serving.

**VARIATIONS:** The sauce can include meat. After the onions, carrots, and celery are cooked, sauté ½ pound of ground beef or beef plus pork. Alternatively, use sweet Italian sausage. Cook the meat over low heat until it is just colored, but don't overcook it or the meat will get hard.

Traditionally, a semisoft pecorino (a sheep's milk cheese) is used. If available, try that or a Spanish Manchego (another kind of soft sheep's milk cheese).

## SAVORY TEFFOLENTA

Contributed by Lynne Fessenden.

In this recipe, teff grain is cooked as you would cook polenta and then fortified with garlic-infused olive oil. Lynne's recipe calls for fresh basil and zucchini, but in the winter, try topping Teffolenta with ratatouille or roasted vegetables.

**¼ cup butter or olive oil**

**8 cloves garlic, minced, divided**

**2 cups teff grain**

**8 cups water**

**1 teaspoon salt**

**1 cup chopped basil, divided**

**6 small zucchini, mixed green and yellow is lovely, sliced into 2-inch strips**

**½ to 1 cup grated Parmesan cheese**

In a skillet, heat a bit of butter or oil and add half of the minced garlic. Cook over medium-low heat, until the aroma is heady and the garlic is softened but not browned. Set aside.

In a large saucepan, bring the water and salt to a boil. Slowly pour the teff into the boiling water, stirring continuously. Simmer for 20 to 25 minutes, stirring often to avoid lumping. When the teff is thick, stir in the garlic-infused olive oil and half of the basil. Pour into a greased 9 x 13-inch glass baking dish. Let stand 1 to 2 hours or refrigerate overnight.

Preheat the oven to 350°F.

Sauté the zucchini with the remaining minced garlic. Stir in the remaining basil. Distribute the zucchini over the cooled teff and top with grated Parmesan cheese. Bake for 30 minutes, until the cheese is melted and the teff is warm.

## WINTER TEFFOLENTA

Top your pan of Teffolenta with a layer of ratatouille — there are many recipes, in fact, there is one in *Eating Close to Home*. Sprinkle with cheese and bake as above. I often make vats of ratatouille at summer's end, when the zucchini, eggplant, peppers, and tomatoes are abundant. It freezes well.

As you can see, Teffolenta is open to many variations. Instead of sautéed zucchini, try a layer of wild mushrooms, roasted vegetables, or Slow-Roasted Tomatoes (page 54) topped with cheese.

## TEFF TIDBITS

* Teff is one of the tiniest grains in the world — only 1/32 of an inch in diameter.
* The word teff comes from Amharic, a Semitic language spoken in Ethiopia. *Teffa* in Amharic means "lost" — an appropriate name for a grain so small!
* 150 teff gains are equal to the size of one kernel of wheat.
* 3000 teff grains weigh only 1 gram.
* One pound of teff seed can yield one ton of harvested grain in only twelve weeks!

## BARLEY MUSHROOM TERRINE

Terrine was originally a French culinary term for chopped meats cooked in layers in an oblong earthenware pan and served cold or at room temperature, as you would pâté. Nowadays, terrines are made with many different ingredients.

Serves 4 to 6.

1½ cups cooked barley, brown rice, or a mixture (see page 111)

1 cup walnuts

2 Tablespoons olive oil

1 medium onion, minced

2 to 3 cloves garlic, minced

½ cup fresh mushrooms, chopped

1 ounce dried wild mushrooms, soaked in boiling water for 20 minutes, drained, and finely minced

1 stalk celery, diced

1 carrot, diced

2 teaspoons chopped fresh thyme or ½ teaspoon dried thyme

1 Tablespoon chopped fresh oregano

1 teaspoon minced fresh sage

2 to 3 eggs, beaten

1 cup cottage cheese

6 ounces grated cheese—I like to use a smoked cheese such as cheddar, gouda, or provolone

Freshly ground pepper

Salt to taste

Smoked or sweet paprika

Romesco Sauce (see page 228)

Preheat the oven to 375°F.

Roast the walnuts in the oven for 5 to 7 minutes, then chop finely.

In a large skillet, heat the olive oil and add the minced onion. Cook until the onion is translucent, then add the garlic, fresh mushrooms, soaked dried mushrooms, celery, carrots, and salt to taste. Cook until the vegetables are tender.

In a large bowl, add the vegetable mixture to the cooked barley and/or rice. Add the herbs, nuts, eggs, cottage cheese, and grated cheese. Mix well, then season to taste with salt and pepper.

Lightly grease a loaf pan, line it with parchment paper, then grease that as well. Let the parchment paper come up over the long sides of the pan so you can use the excess paper as a handle to remove the loaf after it has baked. Pour the batter into the pan and dust the top with paprika. Bake for about 1 hour, until the top is golden and rounded, and the loaf is firm when you give the pan a shake.

Let the loaf sit for 10 minutes or so, then, using the parchment paper handles, lift it out of the pan, and slide the terrine onto a platter. Serve warm, topped with Romesco Sauce.

Leftover terrine is good for lunch, warmed up and served on a bed of lettuce.

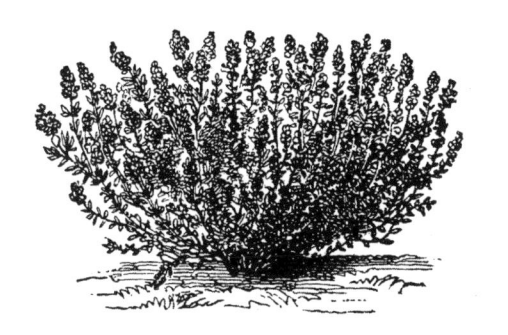

## BUCKWHEAT CRÊPES

Linda Colwell contributed this buckwheat crêpe recipe along with two ideas for filling them. The smoky, nutty, almost mineral quality of the buckwheat flour and the yeastiness of the beer are a perfect foil for upright, bold winter vegetable flavors. And they are equally good with sweet or savory fillings. Linda prefers the lacy, thin quality of crêpes made with all-purpose flour, but I have used whole wheat pastry flour with good results. She also uses a smaller proportion of buckwheat to all-purpose flour than I do. Try it that way, then increase the amount of buckwheat flour as you become accustomed to its taste.

Makes about twenty 6-inch crêpes.

**2 cups milk**

**¼ teaspoon salt**

**½ teaspoon sugar**

**4 Tablespoons butter**

**1 cup all-purpose flour or whole wheat pastry flour**

**¼ cup buckwheat flour, or use up to ¾ cup of buckwheat flour and reduce the amount of wheat flour accordingly, for a total of 1¼ cups**

**1 Tablespoon vegetable oil**

**3 eggs, beaten**

**½ cup beer, preferably an IPA**

**High-heat vegetable oil for cooking**

In a saucepan, combine the milk, salt, sugar, and butter, and heat until the butter melts. Set aside to cool slightly.

In a separate bowl, combine the flours and create a well in the center. Mix the oil and eggs, then pour the egg mixture into the well. Incorporate some of the egg into the sides of the well. As the mixture thickens, add about half of the milk mixture, and whisk until the batter is smooth. Add the remaining milk, whisk, then add the beer, and whisk until smooth. If the batter is lumpy, pour it through a strainer to remove any clumps.

Let the batter sit at room temperature for 1 hour, or you can let it sit overnight in the refrigerator.

Preheat a 6-inch crêpe pan (lacking a crêpe pan, I use a cast-iron pancake griddle), and lightly grease the pan with a high-heat vegetable oil, removing excess oil with a paper towel. Pour a scant ¼ cup of batter into the pan, and quickly swirl the batter around until a thin coat covers the entire bottom. Cook the crêpe until the edges just begin to brown, about a minute. Then, using two small thin spatulas (one on either side of the crêpe), flip the crêpe over and finish cooking the second side.

Stack the finished crêpes on a dinner plate until you fill them, or wrap in plastic and refrigerate if you are using them the next day.

### IDEAS FOR CRÊPE FILLINGS

* Crab and Kale filling (page 140)
* Pear, Prune & Armagnac filling (page 141)
* Sauté chopped spinach with a bit of garlic, and mix it with ricotta cheese, a sprinkling of grated nutmeg, salt and pepper, and a bit of grated Parmesan cheese.
* Chopped ham or prosciutto with grated extra-sharp cheddar or Gruyère cheese.
* Mixed roasted or sautéed vegetables of your choice.
* Sauté apples in butter, sprinkle with nutmeg and cinnamon.
* Spread the crêpes with apple butter or another fruit spread.

Crêpes can be folded as Linda describes on page 140, or rolled with the edges tucked in like a burrito. Or simply spread the filling on half of the crêpe after it has been flipped in the pan, as you would add filling to an omelet. Crêpes are very versatile!

## CRAB AND KALE CRÊPE FILLING

A deceptively simple filling for special occasions during crab season.

Makes 4 servings of 2 crêpes per serving.

**2 to 3 pounds Dungeness crab, or 12 ounces of crab meat**

**1 bunch of kale — Lacinato is good, or use another type**

**2 leeks**

**1 Tablespoon olive oil**

**½ teaspoon of lemon zest**

**Salt**

**Crème fraîche**

Clean the crab and shell the meat. Set aside.

In a pot of boiling salted water, blanch the kale until just tender, about one minute. Refresh in cold water, drain, and squeeze out the excess water. Remove the stems (if you like), coarsely chop the kale, and measure out 2 cups of chopped leaves.

Quarter the leeks lengthwise, then cut thinly crosswise. Rinse the chopped leeks in cold water and drain.

Heat the olive oil in a sauté pan, add the leeks, sprinkle with a little salt, cover, and cook until the leeks are tender. Add the chopped kale and cook for 10 minutes. Remove from heat and add the lemon zest, adjust seasoning, and set aside. Gently heat the crab until just warm.

To assemble, lay a crêpe on a work surface with the first-cooked side up. Spoon an eighth of the leek and kale mixture into the center of the crêpe and spread it across the diameter. Add an eighth of the crab meat on top of the kale, and fold the crêpe over the filling, leaving some of the filling exposed. Repeat for remaining crêpes.

Beat the crème fraîche until soft, and drizzle over the filled crêpes.

## PEAR, PRUNE & ARMAGNAC CRÊPE FILLING

Makes 4 servings of 1 crêpe per serving.

This combination of pears, prunes, honey, and buckwheat crêpes is a great dessert but also makes a wonderful way to start the day. Armagnac is a French brandy; other types of good brandy could stand in for it, or you can leave it out altogether.

**2 russeted pears, such as Taylor's Gold, quartered and cored**

**2 Tablespoons butter**

**2 Tablespoons honey**

**6 prunes soaked in 3 Tablespoons Armagnac (optional), pitted and sliced**
**into quarters**

**Crème fraîche**

Melt the butter in a saucepan, add the honey, prunes, and Armagnac (if using), and sauté for 5 minutes. Add the pear quarters and continue cooking, until the pears are tender but not soft.

To assemble, lay a crêpe on a work surface with the first-cooked side up. Spread a quarter of the pear and prune mixture down the center. Drizzle a couple of spoonfuls of the cooking liquid over the fruit, and fold the crêpe halfway over the filling. Top with a dollop of crème fraîche.

## WHEAT BERRIES ARRABIATA WITH POACHED EGGS

Wheat berries make a great substitute for pasta in many Italian recipes. Here they are cooked with a spicy sauce similar to Italian Arrabiata, and eggs are poached right in the pan to form a complete meal as in the North African dish, *Shakshuka*.

Serves 6 to 8.

**1 cup cooked wheat berries, or try rye berries or oat berries (see page 111)**

**2 to 3 Tablespoons olive oil**

**1 medium onion, finely chopped**

**4 to 5 cloves garlic, minced**

**1 large red pepper, chopped**

**1 teaspoon ground cumin**

**1 Tablespoon smoked paprika**

**¼ teaspoon red pepper flakes**

**¼ cup minced parsley**

**1 quart roasted tomato sauce or fresh, canned, or frozen tomatoes —chop fresh tomatoes and peel if you so desire; crush canned tomatoes; and if using frozen, slip the skins off and quarter them**

**Salt to taste**

**6 to 8 eggs**

**Goat cheese or feta cheese for garnish (optional)**

In a large skillet with steep sides, heat the olive oil and add the onions. Sauté for a few minutes, until the onion is translucent, then add the garlic and red pepper. Continue to sauté until the pepper is tender.

Add the cumin, paprika, red pepper flakes, parsley, and the tomato sauce or tomatoes (with their liquid). Simmer for about 15 minutes, until the sauce thickens slightly. Add the wheat berries and cook for a few minutes more until heated through. Season with salt to taste.

One by one, crack the eggs into a small bowl, then gently slip them into the sauce, arranging them around the pan. Cover the pan and simmer 5 to 10 minutes, until the yolks are set.

Serve right away in bowls, topped with goat cheese or feta cheese, if you desire. To make an even more complete meal, place a nest of steamed greens in the bottom of each bowl.

### HOW TO POACH AN EGG

If you have leftover grains and sauce but no more eggs, it is easy to poach more eggs in water. Here's how.

Add a few inches of water along with a splash of apple cider vinegar or white wine vinegar to a deep skillet or a pot. (The vinegar helps pull the egg together and does not make it taste sour.) Bring the water to a simmer—not a boil! Meanwhile, crack an egg and slide it into a small bowl. When the water is simmering, use a spoon to stir it and get a whirlpool going. Stir with one hand, and slide the egg out of the bowl and into the water with the other. Keep a gentle whirlpool going, and after a minute the egg white will come together around the yolk. Cook for 4 to 5 minutes (you don't have to keep stirring after the egg comes together), until the yolk is set but gives a bit when you poke it gently. Use a slotted spoon to remove the egg to your dish.

## SALMON AND BARLEY CAKES

Contributed by Karen Guillemin

If you have barley already cooked and a tin of locally caught salmon or some leftover grilled salmon, these tasty cakes come together for a quick supper. Leftover cakes make a great lunch the next day. Karen recommends topping the cakes with Mushroom Cream Garnish (page 146). I like the tangy Lemon-Dill Yoghurt Sauce (page 146). Try both!

Makes 12 cakes.

**1 cup golden hulless barley, or substitute hulled barley, sorted and soaked (see page 111)**

**1 Tablespoon butter or olive oil**

**1 medium shallot or ¼ cup onion, finely minced**

**1 egg, beaten**

**2 ounces Gruyère cheese, grated**

**1 Tablespoon minced fresh oregano**

**Salt and freshly ground pepper to taste**

**6-ounce can of skinless, boneless salmon or equal amount cooked salmon**

**1 cup whole wheat panko, divided**

**Olive oil for frying**

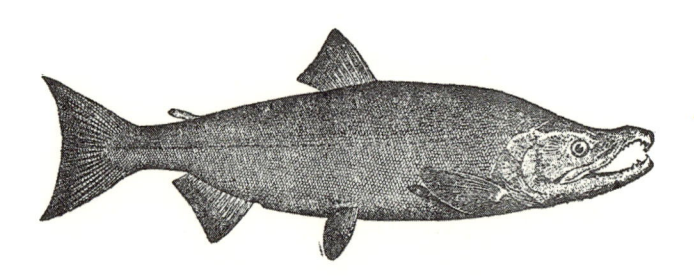

Drain and rinse the soaked barley. Place in a pot with 2 cups of fresh water, bring to a boil, reduce to a simmer, and cook, covered, for about 40 minutes, stirring occasionally. Check the barley for doneness. It will probably need another 5 to 10 minutes to cook; if it is still quite watery, you can remove the lid and let more of the liquid evaporate while the barley finishes cooking. When the barley is tender but still has a firm bite, turn off the heat. Measure out 1 cup of cooked barley and transfer it to a large bowl and allow it to cool. Freeze the remainder for another use.

In a skillet over medium heat, heat the tablespoon of butter or olive oil, and sauté the shallots or onion with a pinch of salt, until very soft but not browned. Add to the barley.

When the barley has cooled, add the egg, Gruyère cheese, oregano, salt, and ground pepper. Break the salmon into flakes with a fork and gently mix it into the batter, along with the juices from the can. If you are using leftover salmon, add a splash of wine if the mixture seems dry.

Now, use your hands to gently mix in about ½ cup of panko; add more if the batter feels too moist. Form the batter into 12 golfball-size balls, then flatten into ½-inch thick patties. Gently press the patties in more panko, and place them on a parchment paper-covered baking sheet. Chill in the refrigerator for at least 30 minutes; this will help the patties firm up and make frying more manageable.

Heat a skillet over medium-high heat. Add about 4 tablespoons of olive oil to generously cover the bottom of the pan. When the oil is shimmering, place half of the cakes into the pan. Leave them alone for a good 5 to 8 minutes, until they are nicely browned. Flip and cook until the second side is nicely browned as well—don't be tempted to flip them too soon.

Serve the cakes on a bed of lettuce that has been tossed with a dressing of olive oil and lemon juice. Pass the Mushroom Cream Garnish and/or the Lemon Yoghurt Dill Sauce.

## MUSHROOM CREAM GARNISH

**8 ounces cremini mushrooms, cleaned and sliced**

**1 Tablespoon butter**

**Salt and pepper**

**¼ cup white vermouth**

**¼ cup crème fraîche**

In a large skillet, over medium heat, melt the butter and sauté the mushrooms with a pinch of salt and plenty of freshly ground black pepper. Let the mushrooms release their juices. Add the vermouth, and continue to sauté until the vermouth has cooked down. Turn off the heat and set aside to cool. When the mushrooms have cooled, put them in a food processor with the crème fraîche and pulse a few times to create a textured paste.

## LEMON-DILL YOGHURT SAUCE

**¾ cup plain yoghurt**

**Juice and zest of one lemon**

**1 to 2 Tablespoons chopped fresh dill**

**¼ teaspoon salt**

Simply mix all ingredients together in a small bowl.

# GRAINS ON THE SIDE... OR ON THE INSIDE!

Along with porridge, a side dish of rice, risotto, or pilaf is perhaps the area to which whole grains most logically lend themselves. Cooked whole grains tossed with butter or olive oil and a handful of minced fresh herbs are a great accompaniment to a variety of meats, a bit of fish, or a slice of frittata. Or instead of pasta, try mixing whole grains with pesto.

Pilaf refers to a dish in which grains are sautéed with onions and other aromatics and then cooked with a broth. Meat and other vegetables can be added as well. It is known in this country as a dish made with rice, but many other grains make wonderful pilaf as well.

Risotto, also, is typically made with rice. In Italy, where the dish originated, white Arborio rice is used. When cooked very slowly with a broth, Arborio rice releases a lot of starch and becomes very creamy. It is often enhanced with butter, Parmesan cheese, and a variety of seasonal vegetables.

As it happens, many other whole grains make equally creamy risotto. Short-grain brown rice, as well as short-grain red and black rice, all contain the type of starch that results in a creamy texture, particularly if soaked overnight. Barley makes a wonderful risotto, as does farro. Oat berries, spelt berries, and other types of wheat berries can also stand in for rice.

Flavored grains or pilaf can be used to stuff a variety of vegetables. Consider stuffing bell peppers, zucchini, or winter squash. Roll some risotto or pilaf in a few cabbage leaves and simmer them in tomato sauce. You don't have to limit yourself to stuffing vegetables, either! A chicken stuffed with whole grains makes a wonderful Sunday dinner.

## GOLDEN BARLEY RISOTTO WITH WILD MUSHROOMS

Serves 6 to 8.

**1 cup golden hulless barley, sorted and soaked (see page 111)**

**1 cup dried mushrooms—porcini, shiitake, morel, or other wild mushrooms, or a mixture**

**¼ pound fresh chanterelle mushrooms, cleaned and chopped into ½-inch pieces, or substitute other fresh mushrooms, depending on the season and what is available**

**2 Tablespoons olive oil**

**½ cup finely chopped onion**

**1 large clove garlic, minced**

**½ cup white wine**

**½ teaspoon fresh lemon zest**

**1 pinch red pepper flakes**

**½ teaspoon fresh thyme, minced**

**Salt and pepper to taste**

**½ cup parsley, chopped**

**½ cup grated Parmesan cheese**

Drain and rinse the soaked barley. Place in a large pot with a scant 3 cups of fresh water. Bring to a boil, turn down to a simmer, and cook, covered, stirring occasionally, for 40 to 45 minutes, until just tender and the liquid has been absorbed.

While the barley is simmering, rinse the dried mushrooms and soak them in 2 cups of boiling water, until soft. Squeeze the liquid out of the mushrooms, and reserve it to use for stock. Mince the mushrooms and set aside.

Next, sauté the fresh mushrooms. Chanterelles do well with a dry sauté: heat a cast-iron skillet, sprinkle salt in it, then add the mushrooms. Cook over medium heat, for 5 to 10 minutes, until the mushrooms have released their liquid and it has evaporated. Alternatively, you can sauté the mushrooms in butter. Either way, after the fresh mushrooms are cooked, add the minced, dried mushrooms and remove from the heat.

In a large saucepan, heat the oil over medium heat, and add the onion. Cook, stirring, until tender, then add the garlic. Cook another few minutes, until the garlic is fragrant but not browned. Stir in the barley and the wine. Cook until the wine has evaporated, stirring often. Add the mushroom stock and simmer, stirring often, until most of the liquid has evaporated, about 20 minutes. If the liquid absorbs completely before the barley is very tender, add hot water, half a cup at a time.

When most of the liquid has evaporated and the barley is very creamy, add the mushrooms, lemon zest, red pepper flakes, and minced thyme. Mix well and add salt and pepper to taste. Stir in the parsley and Parmesan cheese. Remove from the heat and enjoy!

**NOTE:** You can skip the step of pre-cooking the barley by adding the soaked barley to the sautéed onions and garlic. You'll need to add more liquid, and it will take 45 to 55 minutes or longer to reach the creamy risotto-like stage.

**VARIATIONS:** After the risotto is cooked, you can add other vegetables along with the mushrooms. Peas are traditional, but roasted root vegetables would go well, as would small cubes of cooked winter squash. Sun-dried tomatoes might be a nice addition. Just make sure the vegetables are cooked and chopped into small pieces or sliced thin. You might also try substituting feta cheese or other goat cheese for the Parmesan.

Or try other grains, such as farro.

## ITALIAN SUPPLI

*Suppli* (pronounced *soo*-plee) are an Italian snack made from risotto. You can use leftover risotto or cook up a pot specifically for the purpose—they are certainly tasty enough to warrant it!

**2 cups Golden Barley Risotto (see page 148)**

**Approximately 6 ounces of mozzarella or other good melting cheese, such as fontina, cut into small cubes**

**1 to 2 eggs**

**Breadcrumbs**

**6 Tablespoons olive oil**

Form a ball of risotto, about the size of a plum. Holding the ball in the palm of your hand, press a piece of cheese into the middle, then reshape. Transfer to a plate or baking sheet and form the rest of the suppli.

Beat the egg in a shallow bowl, and spread the breadcrumbs on a plate. Dip each suppli in the egg, then roll in the breadcrumbs until well coated.

In a heavy skillet, heat the olive oil and fry the suppli, a few at a time, until golden brown on all sides. Drain on a paper towel. Serve hot or at room temperature.

**VARIATIONS:** Instead of cheese you can stuff the suppli with bits of meat or vegetables or a bit of meat mixed with tomato sauce. A more traditional risotto made with Arborio rice will work just as well as Barley Risotto.

## WHEAT BERRY PILAF

Adapted from a recipe contributed by Open Oak Farms.

Serves 6 to 8.

**2 cups wheat berries, sorted and soaked (see page 111)**

**4 to 5 cups vegetable stock, chicken stock, or water**

**5 Tablespoons olive oil**

**1 to 2 Tablespoons balsamic or apple cider vinegar**

**1 Tablespoon lemon juice**

**2 cloves garlic, minced**

**½ cup chopped, toasted hazelnuts or almonds**

**¼ cup chopped scallions**

**½ cup minced parsley**

**Salt and pepper to taste**

**½ cup feta or queso fresco-type cheese**

Drain the soaked wheat berries. Place in a large pot and toast over medium-high heat, until the wheat berries are fragrant. Add the water or stock, carefully, as it may splatter. Bring to a boil, then cover, and turn down to a simmer. Cook for 30 to 45 minutes, until tender but not too mushy. Drain off any unabsorbed liquid.

In a large bowl whisk together the olive oil, vinegar, lemon juice, and garlic. Add this to the wheat berries, along with the nuts, scallions, and parsley. Mix well. Season with salt and pepper if desired, and fold in the cheese. Serve warm.

**VARIATION:** You could substitute any number of grain berries, such as oat or rye berries, in this dish.

## WILD RICE WITH CRANBERRIES AND CARAMELIZED ONIONS

Adapted from a recipe by Running Wild Rice of Brownsville, Oregon. Serves 4 to 6.

**2 cups chicken or vegetable stock**

**1 cup wild rice, or half wild rice and half brown rice**

**3 Tablespoons olive oil**

**1 large onion, cut in half and sliced into very thin half-moons**

**1 teaspoon minced fresh sage, rosemary, and thyme, in whatever combination you prefer**

**½ cup dried cranberries**

**½ teaspoon lemon zest**

**½ cup chopped fresh parsley**

**¼ cup chopped, toasted hazelnuts**

In a medium saucepan, combine the stock and rice. Bring to a boil, then reduce heat to a simmer. Cover and cook, 45 to 60 minutes, until the rice is tender and the liquid has been absorbed.

Meanwhile, heat the oil in a medium-size skillet. Add the onions and fresh herbs and cook over medium-low heat, until the onions are very soft and translucent and golden. Stir in the cranberries, cover the pan, and let the berries soften.

When the rice is done, fold in the cranberry-onion mixture, the lemon zest, fresh parsley, and toasted hazelnuts. Serve as a side dish, or try it as a stuffing for baked delicata or other small winter squash.

Leftovers are very good tossed into a salad the next day.

# Grain Salads

Cooked whole grains are a great way to enhance a mixed green salad. They also serve well as a base for a more complex salad. Easily improvised, the basic structure of a grain salad is thus:

Start with cooked grains: figure on two cups of uncooked grain to serve six to eight people. Consider flavoring the grain with herbs or spices as it cooks. If you are using leftover grain, gently warm it before you proceed with the salad.

Toss the warm grain with the dressing of your choice. A simple dressing of olive oil and lemon, orange, or lime juice (or a combination) works well. Alternatively, use balsamic or sherry or champagne vinegar if you have one of those on hand. Mix spices, such as smoked paprika or Ancho chile powder, into the dressing.

A light curry dressing is another good way to go. Whisk together 2 tablespoons of lemon juice, 2 teaspoons of rice vinegar or cider vinegar, 1 teaspoon of curry powder, and 4 tablespoons of olive oil. Season to taste with salt and pepper, and add more curry powder if you like.

Now add some vegetables. You can mix raw veggies with those that have been lightly steamed. Warm grain salads pair well with roasted vegetables. Bits of dried fruit are fun, especially tart fruit like cranberries or tart cherries.

Toasted nuts and seeds should be added just before serving, so they don't absorb the dressing and get soggy.

Definitely toss in a heaping helping of chopped fresh herbs such as parsley, dill, chives, cilantro, or basil. Add salt and pepper to taste, garnish with grated Parmesan cheese or crumbles of feta or goat cheese, and you've got the basis of a great meal!

## PURPLE BARLEY SALAD WITH APPLE AND CELERY

The deep rich flavor of purple barley is set off by the bright flavors and crunch of apple and fennel.

Serves 4 to 8.

1 cup purple hulless barley, sorted and soaked (see page 111)

1 sprig thyme

1 large bay leaf

1 strip of lemon peel

1 large apple, chopped into ½-inch pieces

1 fennel bulb, cut lengthwise and sliced into very thin half-moons

2 stalks celery, chopped

½ cup scallions, minced

½ cup dried cranberries

¼ cup minced fresh dill, or substitute 1 to 2 teaspoons dried dill

¼ cup minced fresh parsley

1 teaspoon ground coriander

3 Tablespoons olive oil

¼ cup lemon juice (the juice of 1 large lemon)

1 teaspoon lemon zest

Chopped, toasted walnuts or hazelnuts (optional)

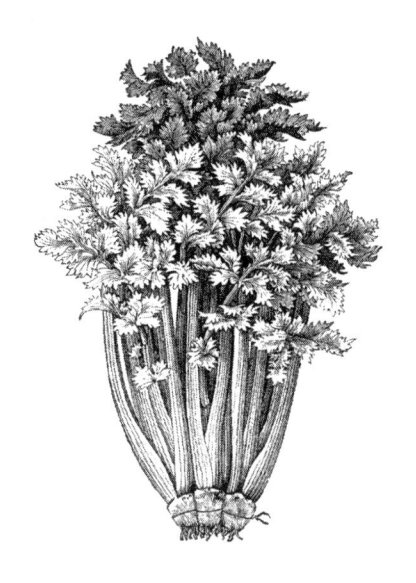

Drain and rinse the soaked barley. Place in a large pot with a scant 3 cups of fresh water. Tie the thyme, bay leaf, and lemon peel into a bit of cheesecloth and add that to the pot. Bring to a boil, turn down to a simmer, and cook, covered, stirring occasionally, for 30 to 45 minutes, until the barley is just tender and the liquid has been absorbed. Remove the cheesecloth bag.

In a large bowl, combine the apple, fennel, celery, scallions, cranberries, dill, parsley, and coriander. Mix well. Toss with the barley while it is still warm. Whisk together the olive oil, lemon juice, and lemon zest. Add to the barley and mix again. Let the salad stand for 15 to 20 minutes, so the barley absorbs the flavors. Season to taste with salt and pepper. Serve at room temperature on a bed of greens. Sprinkle with chopped toasted nuts if desired.

**VARIATION:** Toss the sliced fennel bulb with some olive oil and a bit of salt. Spread on a rimmed baking sheet, and bake at 425°F, for about 15 minutes, until it is tender and starting to caramelize.

GRAIN SALADS

## ROAST ROOTS 'N RYE

A winter salad.

Serves 4 to 8.

**2 to 3 cups cooked rye berries (see page 111)**

**1 medium onion, cut into ½-inch chunks**

**2 carrots, cut into ½-inch chunks**

**1 to 2 parsnips, cut into ½-inch chunks**

**Olive oil**

**1 bunch of kale or other winter green of your choice — arugula, mustard, spinach, chard — center ribs removed and cut into 1-inch pieces**

**1 Tablespoon balsamic vinegar**

**1 Tablespoon lemon juice**

**3 Tablespoons olive oil**

**1 teaspoon Dijon mustard**

**Salt and pepper to taste**

**½ cup dried cranberries**

**1 cup chopped fresh parsley**

**Goat cheese or mild creamy feta**

Preheat the oven to 450°F.

Toss the onion, carrots, and parsnips with a tablespoon or two of olive oil, sprinkle with salt, and spread on a rimmed baking sheet. Bake for 12 to 15 minutes, until the vegetables are tender and starting to caramelize.

In a bowl, toss the kale with a tablespoon or two of olive oil, sprinkle with salt. When the other vegetables are just shy of being roasted to your liking, spread the greens on top and return the pan to the oven. Roast for an additional minute or two. If you are using a tender green such as spinach or mustard, skip this step.

Warm the cooked rye berries. Whisk together the vinegar, lemon juice, olive oil, and mustard. Add salt and pepper to taste. Place the rye berries in a large bowl with the dressing and toss to coat. Add the roasted vegetables and toss again. If you are using tender greens, add them at this point—the heat of the roasted vegetables and the warm rye berries will wilt them. Add the cranberries, chopped parsley, and goat or feta cheese.

Serve warm or at room temperature.

**VARIATIONS:** Add cubes of peeled winter squash to the carrots and parsnips. Add or substitute other root vegetables, such as rutabagas or celery root. Try other dried fruit, such as currants instead of the cranberries. Top with toasted nuts, or toss in some smoked salmon. Instead of greens, you could use steamed broccoli, or you could roast halved Brussels sprouts with the other vegetables.

GRAIN SALADS

## WHEAT BERRY SALAD WITH BROCCOLI, APPLE, HAZELNUTS & SMOKED SALMON

A complete meal in a bowl!

Serves 4 to 8.

**2 cups wheat berries, sorted and soaked (see page 111)**

**1 large head of broccoli**

**2 stalks celery, finely diced**

**1 large crisp tart apple, cored and chopped**

**1 cup chopped parsley—Italian flat leaf is best**

**½ pound smoked salmon, broken into small pieces**

**1 cup roughly chopped, toasted hazelnuts**

**6 Tablespoons olive oil**

**¼ cup lemon juice (the juice of 1 large lemon)**

**1 clove garlic, finely minced or pressed**

**1 teaspoon Dijon mustard**

**Salt and pepper to taste**

Drain the soaked wheat berries. Place in a large pot with 4 cups of fresh water. Bring to a boil, turn down to a simmer, cover, and cook, about 30 minutes, until tender but still intact and chewy. Remove from the heat and drain. If you don't have time to soak the berries overnight, increase the cooking time to 45 minutes to 1 hour.

While the wheat berries are cooking, cut the stems off the broccoli, and peel and chop the stem. Break the heads into small bite-size florets. Steam the broccoli, until just tender but still bright green. Immediately run under cold water or plunge it into a bowl of ice water to stop the cooking process.

Whisk together the olive oil, lemon juice, garlic, mustard, salt, and pepper. In a large bowl, toss together the wheat berries, broccoli, celery, apple, parsley, and the dressing. Just prior to serving, mix in the smoked fish and the hazelnuts. Can be served at room temperature or chilled.

**VARIATIONS:** The smoked salmon can be omitted altogether or replaced with smoked trout, tuna, or other forms of protein. Dried cranberries are a nice addition. Seasonal vegetables can replace the broccoli; asparagus and/or fresh peas in the spring, or try lightly steamed zucchini and halved cherry tomatoes in the summer. A bit of fresh goat cheese sprinkled on top is very tasty. Substitute wild rice for all or some of the wheat berries.

### HAZELNUTS ROASTING ON AN OPEN FIRE?

You don't have to crack hazelnuts before you roast them! Bake unshelled hazelnuts at 275°F, for 20 minutes or so, until they smell nice and toasty. Remove to a bowl to cool a bit before you go at them with your nutcracker. Or toss unshelled hazelnuts into a cast-iron pan and cook them over medium heat, shaking the pan periodically, until the nuts are deep brown all over. Toasting over an open fire might be tricky, but hazelnuts in a vegetable basket over your grill would work!

## SUMMER GRAIN SALAD

Similar to tabbouleh, but with whole grains instead of bulgur wheat. Serves 4 to 8.

**1 cup golden hulless barley, farro, Kamut, frikeh, or wheat berries, or a mixture, sorted and soaked (see page 111)**

**3 Tablespoons olive oil**

**3 Tablespoons lemon juice**

**3 cloves garlic, pressed**

**Salt to taste**

**½ cup chopped fresh parsley**

**¼ to ½ cup chopped fresh mint**

**½ cup minced sweet onion, or substitute scallions**

**1 bunch radishes, sliced thinly**

**1 cucumber, peeled and diced**

**1 red pepper, diced**

**1 to 2 fresh tomatoes, chopped**

**2 Tablespoons capers**

**Kalamata olives**

**Feta cheese**

Drain and rinse the soaked grain. Place in a large pot with 3 cups of fresh water. Bring to a boil, turn down to a simmer, and cook, covered, until just tender and the water has been absorbed, about 30 to 45 minutes.

Mix together the olive oil, lemon juice, garlic, and salt to taste. In a large bowl, pour this dressing over the warm grain. Allow the grain to absorb the dressing while it cools a bit, then add the parsley, mint, onions or scallions, radishes, cucumber, red pepper, and tomatoes. Toss well and serve at room temperature on a bed of lettuce, garnished with capers, Kalamata olives, and crumbled feta cheese.

# GRAIN SOUPS AND STEWS

Chicken soup with rice, beef and barley stew, and Scotch broth are some well-known soups that incorporate whole grains. As you might expect, there are many other ways to bring grains into a warm bowl on a chilly winter night! And grain soups don't have to be steaming, either—try a chilled Buttermilk and Frikeh Soup (page 166) on a warm summer evening.

> **TOP THAT!**
>
> Need to jazz up your soup? Instead of reaching for croutons, try Fried Garbanzo Beans (page 36), a dollop of Walnut-Olive Spread (page 225), or a swirl of parsley, arugula, or basil pesto (pages 79, 169, 227).
>
> Or make some kale chips to scatter over your bowl of soup! Take a bunch of lacinato kale (also called dinosaur kale) —about 6 ounces—remove the stems and cut or tear the leaves into large chunks. Toss the kale in a bowl with a tablespoon of olive oil and salt to taste. Spread the pieces on a rimmed baking sheet, and bake at 300°F, until the kale is nice and crispy, about 20 minutes. Mmm good!

## BARLEY BEEF STEW WITH MUSHROOMS

A hearty stew full of rich winter vegetables.

Serves 6 to 8, easily.

**4 cups cooked golden hulless barley (see page 111)**

**½ pound beef stew meat, cut into ½-inch cubes (optional)**

**2 Tablespoons olive oil, divided**

**1 onion, chopped**

**1 large clove garlic, minced**

**3 medium carrots, diced**

**2 stalks celery, diced**

**2 small parsnips, peeled and diced**

**½ pound fresh mushrooms — wild or domestic — chopped**

**6 cups stock — beef stock is good, chicken stock is fine, mushroom stock is wonderful**

**1 bay leaf**

**1 teaspoon minced fresh thyme**

**⅛ teaspoon red pepper flakes**

**1 pound kale, center ribs removed and cut into bite-size pieces**

**4 Tablespoons tomato paste**

**2 Tablespoons cider vinegar**

**Salt and pepper to taste**

If using beef, season it with salt and pepper. In a large soup pot, heat 1 tablespoon of the olive oil over medium heat, and add the beef (you might need to do this in batches so the cubes are not crowded). Brown the meat, remove, and set aside.

In the same pot, heat the remaining olive oil, and sauté the onions over medium-low heat until they are softened. Stir in the garlic, carrots, celery, parsnips, and mushrooms. Cook, stirring often, for 5 minutes or so, until the vegetables start to release their juices.

Add the meat back to the pot, along with the stock, bay leaf, thyme, and red pepper flakes. Bring to a boil, reduce the heat, and simmer, covered, until the meat is tender, about 30 minutes. Add the kale and cooked barley, and stir in the tomato paste. Simmer another 20 minutes, until everything is tender. Add the cider vinegar and salt and pepper to taste.

**VARIATIONS:** If you prefer not to use beef, consider adding a cup or more of cooked beans toward the end of the cooking time. Another alternative to beef could be lamb, in which case, it would be appropriate to add some fresh minced dill at the end.

## BULGUR WHEAT SOUP WITH LENTILS AND WINTER GREENS

Bulgur and lentils are both quick cooking, as neither needs to be pre-soaked, making this a great soup to put together midweek.

Serves 6 to 8.

1 cup lentils, sorted and rinsed

1 cup bulgur wheat

6 to 8 cups water or stock

2 cloves garlic, minced

¼ teaspoon red pepper flakes

½ teaspoon smoked paprika

1 bay leaf

½ cup minced parsley

4 Tablespoons olive oil, divided

1 medium onion, finely chopped

1 large carrot, finely diced

1 stalk celery, finely diced

2 cups kale—or substitute other greens such as mustard greens or chard—center ribs removed and cut into short ribbons

2 Tablespoons cider vinegar

Salt and pepper to taste

Soft goat cheese

In a soup pot, combine the lentils with the bulgur wheat, water or stock, garlic, red pepper flakes, smoked paprika, bay leaf, and parsley. Bring to a boil, then lower the heat, and simmer with the lid slightly ajar.

While the lentils and bulgur wheat are cooking, heat half of the oil in a skillet and sauté the onions over low heat, stirring occasionally, until they soften. Add the carrot and celery and continue to cook, about 10 minutes, until the onions are golden brown and the carrot and celery are tender. Add the cooked vegetables to the soup pot.

In the same skillet, heat the remaining 2 tablespoons of oil and sauté the greens until they are tender. Cooking time will vary depending on the greens you choose—kale takes about 5 to 10 minutes, chard or mustard greens take somewhat less time. Add the cooked greens to the pot, and continue to cook the soup, until the lentils and bulgur wheat are tender and the flavors have become well acquainted. Just before serving, remove the bay leaf, stir in the vinegar, and add salt and pepper to taste. Top each bowl with some crumbled, soft goat cheese.

## FRIKEH AND BUTTERMILK SOUP

Carol Boutard, of Ayers Creek Farm outside of Portland, contributed this recipe which highlights frikeh, a toasted wheat berry that she and her husband, Anthony, produce and sell at the Hillsdale Farmers Market. The soup is based on Deborah Madison's buttermilk and barley soup and Portland chef Kelly Meyers' version, which substitutes frikeh for barley.

Frikeh is made by harvesting wheat when it is still green, burning it to stop the conversion from sugar to starch, and then threshing the grain from the head. The process produces a jade-green grain that is slightly charred and has a sweet smoky quality. If you cannot find frikeh, bulgur wheat would be a good substitute, although it will not have the characteristic smoky flavor.

Serve chilled, garnished with purslane tops. Purslane is a slightly sweet, lemony, spicy green that also happens to be chock full of omega-3 fatty acids and other wonderful things for your body. If you don't have access to purslane, try a scattering of chopped baby arugula leaves. Nasturtium blossoms, with their fragrant spiciness, might be good, too.

### MORE FUN WITH FRIKEH

* Use frikeh in salads, such as the Wheat Berry Salad on page 158. Or in place of bulgur wheat for a smoky twist on tabbouleh salad.
* Make a frikeh pilaf to tuck up next to (or inside of) a roast chicken. Sauté a chopped onion in a few tablespoons of olive oil. Add 1 cup of frikeh, 2 cups of water or stock, a cardamom pod or two, a bay leaf, and a dash of cinnamon and allspice. Bring to a boil, then reduce to a simmer. Cook, covered, until tender, about 35 to 45 minutes. Season with salt and pepper, and maybe a bit of lemon zest.

Serves 4 to 6.

**2 cups frikeh**

**¼ cup minced spring onion**

**2 Tablespoons minced fresh dill**

**1 Tablespoon minced fresh cilantro**

**1 teaspoon ground coriander, toasted**

**1 quart buttermilk**

**1 cup lightly chopped, young purslane tops**

**Salt to taste**

Rinse the frikeh well in a couple of changes of water, and skim off any floaters and errant bits of hull or chaff. Cook the frikeh in salted boiling water until tender, about 35 to 45 minutes. Drain and add the spring onion, dill, cilantro, coriander, and the buttermilk. Chill completely. Just before serving, add the purslane tops and salt to taste. The soup will have the consistency of a cold vegetable stew. If you prefer a thinner soup, add a bit of vegetable or chicken stock.

**VARIATION:** Serve the soup warm, but don't reheat to the point of boiling after you add the buttermilk or it will separate.

GRAIN SOUPS AND STEWS

## MINESTRONE WITH WHEAT BERRIES AND ARUGULA PESTO

Wheat berries stand in for pasta in this version of minestrone, and a dollop of arugula pesto instead of the traditional basil pesto adds a unique twist.

Serves 6 to 8.

**2 cups cooked Cranberry beans (see page 29)**

**1 cup cooked wheat berries or other grain of your choice (see page 111)**

**3 Tablespoons olive oil**

**1 onion, chopped**

**2 to 3 cloves garlic, minced**

**1 to 2 carrots, minced**

**1 to 2 stalks celery, minced**

**5 cups vegetable or chicken stock**

**1 bay leaf**

**1 cup green beans, cut into small pieces**

**½ head green cabbage, shredded**

**2 cups chopped tomatoes—fresh, frozen, or canned**

**1 to 2 zucchini, chopped**

**½ cup minced parsley**

**¼ cup chopped basil**

**Salt and pepper to taste**

**Arugula Pesto for topping**

Heat the oil in a large soup pot. Sauté the onion until translucent, then add the garlic, carrots, and celery, and sauté until all the vegetables are softened. Add the stock and bay leaf, bring to a boil, and reduce to a simmer. Add the green beans, cabbage, and tomatoes and simmer until almost tender. Add the zucchini and parsley and simmer until the vegetables are cooked but not mushy. Add the basil, Cranberry beans, wheat berries, and salt and pepper to taste. Keep warm.

**VARIATIONS:** Play with other vegetable combinations. More root vegetables, such as parsnip, turnip, rutabaga, and celeriac would be great in the winter when zucchini is not available. A bit of fresh fennel would be tasty. Add a few shakes of red pepper flakes to give the soup a bit of bite. And, of course, basil pesto is great instead of Arugula Pesto.

### ARUGULA PESTO

**3 cloves garlic**

**½ teaspoon salt**

**2 cups arugula leaves**

**½ cup parsley**

**⅓ cup olive oil**

**½ cup grated Parmesan cheese**

**2 to 3 Tablespoons lemon juice**

Place all ingredients in a food processor and process until smooth. Remove to a bowl and pass at the table.

## SMOKY TOMATO SOUP WITH QUINOA

A light soup that would be good as a first course.

Serves 6 to 8.

3 cups cooked quinoa (see page 113)

3 Tablespoons olive oil

1 small onion, finely minced

1 stalk celery, finely minced

1 Tablespoon smoked Ancho chile powder

1 teaspoon ground coriander

1 teaspoon ground cumin

1 teaspoon smoked paprika

1 teaspoon minced fresh thyme or ½ teaspoon dried thyme

1 bay leaf

2 to 3 Tablespoons tomato paste

2 pounds fresh or frozen tomatoes, roughly chopped — slip the skins off frozen tomatoes by briefly immersing them in hot water

4 cups chicken or vegetable stock

1½ Tablespoons sugar

1 teaspoon salt, or to taste

Freshly ground pepper to taste

Zest of 1 lemon

Chopped cilantro

Goat cheese or Cotija cheese

In a soup pot, heat the olive oil over medium heat, and add the onion and celery. Sauté slowly until the onion and celery are very soft but not browned. Add the spices, thyme, and bay leaf and sauté a few more minutes, until the spices are fragrant.

Stir in the tomato paste, tomatoes, chicken or vegetable stock, sugar, salt, and pepper, and bring to a boil. Reduce to a simmer and cook until the tomatoes have fallen apart, 15 to 20 minutes. Remove the bay leaf.

At this point, you can put the soup through a food mill to remove the skins and seeds, or you can purée with an immersion blender. Or just leave it as is, but press the larger chunks of tomato against the side of the pot with a wooden spoon to mash them a bit.

Add the quinoa and lemon zest. Simmer until just heated through. Taste and adjust seasonings. You can add a pinch of cayenne pepper (or smoked cayenne pepper flakes) if you want more of a bite. Fresh lemon juice can be added, as well.

Serve warm, topped with chopped cilantro and a bit of tangy goat cheese or Mexican Cotija cheese.

**VARIATIONS:** Use canned fire-roasted tomatoes, instead of fresh or frozen tomatoes. Rice, particularly wild rice, is tasty in lieu of quinoa.

## WINTER SQUASH STEW WITH PURPLE BARLEY

Ground sesame seeds and almonds are used to thicken and enrich this hearty, smoky stew.

Serves 6 to 8.

**1 to 2 cups cooked purple barley, depending on how many people you are serving and how hearty you want the stew to be (see page 111)**

**1 cup cooked white beans or pinto beans—try Indian Woman Yellow, Brightstone, or Yellow-Eyed beans (see page 29)**

**1½ teaspoons cumin seeds**

**2 teaspoons dried oregano**

**3 Tablespoons sesame seeds**

**¼ cup almonds**

**2 Tablespoons olive oil**

**1 large onion, chopped**

**2 large cloves garlic, minced**

**2 Tablespoons chile powder**

**1 Tablespoon smoked Ancho chile powder**

**1 large butternut squash or 3 cups other winter squash, cut into ¾-inch chunks**

**3 cups water, broth, or juice from tomatoes, or a mixture**

**1 small head cauliflower, broken into small bite-size pieces**

**2 pounds tomatoes—fresh, frozen, or canned—chopped, with juice reserved**

**¼ cup minced parsley**

**2 Tablespoons chopped cilantro or more to taste**

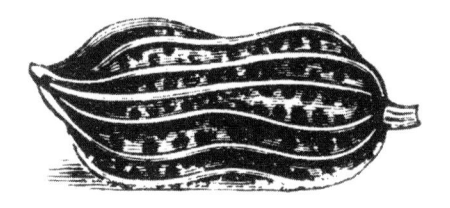

In a small dry cast-iron skillet, toast the cumin seeds over medium heat for several minutes, until they begin to darken and the aroma deepens. Stir the seeds or shake the pan frequently while you are toasting so that they don't burn. Remove to a bowl. In the same skillet, toast the sesame seeds until lightly browned, stirring or shaking them as well. Set the sesame seeds aside, and finally, in the same skillet, toast the almonds until lightly browned. Remove the almonds to a cutting board and chop them roughly. Now put the toasted cumin and the oregano in a spice mill and grind to a powder. Remove to a bowl and set aside. In the same mill, grind the sesame seeds and almonds together into a fine meal and set aside.

In a large stew pot or casserole dish, heat the oil over medium heat and add the onions. Sauté until they begin to soften, then add the garlic, cumin-oregano mixture, and both chile powders. Cook for another minute. Add the squash and the 3 cups of liquid. Bring to a boil, then lower the heat, cover, and cook slowly, for about 20 minutes, until the squash is tender.

When the squash is fork tender, add the ground sesame seeds and almonds, along with the cooked barley and beans, cauliflower, and the tomatoes. Season with salt to taste, and add more chile powder, if desired. Cook until the cauliflower is just tender, then add the parsley and cilantro. Simmer a few more minutes, until all the flavors are well acquainted.

Serve with sour cream or grated sharp cheddar cheese, and a sprinkling of chopped cilantro.

# EASY BAKED GOODS

Making bread—yeasted bread that is—is a satisfying albeit lengthy process of turning ground grain into the staff of life. There are many wonderful books that describe how to make a good loaf of bread. Recently, Jim Lahy developed a technique for no-knead bread that utilizes a long rising period and can be quite adaptable to busy schedules. Fermented bread, or sourdough, can be similarly easy to work into one's day-to-day routine. There are a couple of types of bread, Limpa (page 202) and Sourdough Rye (page 206), I make with some frequency. On a daily or weekly basis, however, baking bread requires a time commitment that I, like many, am often not able to meet. Fortunately, there are many other ways to use whole grain flour!

Start with your basic mixture of flour and water—which is what I imagine people did all those many years ago when they started grinding grains. Mix corn flour and water, put it on a hot surface, and you get a tortilla; wheat flour and water yields a flatbread; variations of these can be found in many different cultures. Combine flour, water, and a bit of butter or oil, roll it out very thin, put it in an oven, and you get crackers! Quick, easy, and very satisfying—crackers are a great way to start incorporating locally grown whole wheat flours into your diet.

Quick breads are another way to go. Think muffins, soda bread, and biscuits, all of which use a leavening agent other than yeast, such as baking powder or baking soda, often mixed with yoghurt or buttermilk.

It is fun to play with flours made from different types of grain. Mixing whole grain flours with unbleached white flour can make it easier to introduce these new flavors to your palate. Rye, spelt, oats, barley, and Kamut are all available as flour, and all have a unique personality and flavor. Even within each grain type, there are variations. Wheat flour made from hard red wheat, for instance, is quite different from that made from soft spring wheat. Bakers with discerning palates are said to be able to taste the difference between a hard red wheat grown in one area of the Pacific Northwest from another—much as a wine connoisseur can taste the difference between a California pinot noir and an Oregon pinot noir.

## CORN CRISPS, CORN PONES & SPOONBREAD

Ground corn is used in place of wheat flour in many cultures and was a staple for the early European settlers in the U.S., who did not have access to wheat. The following recipes have as their foundation a simple mixture of ground corn and boiling water (or boiling milk in the case of spoonbread). Made from locally grown heirloom corn, these recipes are fragrant, satisfying, and simple to make.

### CORN CRISPS

A family favorite from the '60s.

**1 cup medium-grind cornmeal**

**½ teaspoon salt**

**1½ cups boiling water**

**¼ cup melted butter**

Preheat the oven to 350°F.

In a mixing bowl, stir together the cornmeal and salt, then whisk in the boiling water and butter. Drop by the tablespoon onto a well-oiled baking sheet and spread thin (about ¼-inch thick or less) with the back of the spoon. Bake for 20 minutes, until the edges are lightly browned, and they are crisp but not too dark. Serve hot—with more butter if you are so inclined. Excellent with split pea soup.

## CORN PONES

Corn pones were traditionally made in something like a muffin pan, but instead being muffin-shaped, the openings were half-cylinders, roughly the size of a corn cob. Later corn pone pans had openings that were actually shaped like ears of corn, kernels and all. Corn pones have long been a staple of Southern U.S. cooking and have been discussed by many American writers, including Mark Twain.

Andrea Davis of King Valley Gardens shared this recipe, which she makes from her own homegrown corn ground in a Vita-Mix.

**3 cups cornmeal**

**½ teaspoon salt**

**2 cups boiling water**

**⅓ cup oil**

Preheat the oven to 375°F.

In a mixing bowl, thoroughly stir together the cornmeal and salt. Add the boiling water and oil to the cornmeal mixture. Mix well. If the mixture is very dry, add more water, but do not add too much —use just enough water to make a firm dough. Let the dough rest until it has cooled down substantially, at least 15 minutes. Form into about 15 pones, about ¼-inch thick rectangles. You can either bake them for about 20 minutes, on an oiled baking sheet, until the edges start to brown, or if you are in a hurry or cooking on a wood stove, fry them in a frying pan.

## SPOONBREAD

This was another staple when I was growing up in upstate New York. Not really a bread, it is closer to a soufflé, but a bit more substantial.

**2 cups milk, divided**

**1 cup medium-grind cornmeal**

**1 teaspoon salt**

**3 Tablespoons butter, melted**

**4 eggs, separated**

**1 teaspoon baking powder**

Preheat the oven to 375°F.

In a saucepan, bring 1 cup of the milk to a boil, then whisk in the cornmeal and salt. Stir for a minute, then remove from the heat. Add the melted butter and stir well, then whisk in the egg yolks, baking powder, and the remaining cup of cold milk. Pour into a soufflé dish.

Beat the egg whites until they form stiff peaks, and fold them into the batter. Place the soufflé dish in a larger pan filled with water, and bake for 35 to 40 minutes, until set.

## SPICY NUTTY APPLE RYE MUFFINS

Muffins are a great way to start using different whole grain flours, and they are a fairly easy type of recipe to improvise with. Embellish them with your favorite fruits, nuts, and spices. Or top them with Cinnamon Streusel for a special treat.

Makes a dozen muffins.

**1 cup whole wheat flour or whole wheat pastry flour**

**1 cup rye flour**

**½ teaspoon salt**

**1 teaspoon baking powder**

**½ teaspoon baking soda**

**¼ cup brown sugar**

**1 teaspoon cinnamon**

**½ teaspoon ground ginger**

**¼ teaspoon ground nutmeg**

**⅛ teaspoon each: ground cloves and allspice**

**1 cup buttermilk**

**2 small eggs, beaten**

**1 teaspoon vanilla**

**½ cup melted butter, cooled somewhat**

**2 cups minced fresh apple**

**½ cup finely chopped, toasted hazelnuts**

Preheat the oven to 375°F.

In a large bowl, mix the dry ingredients well; it is not necessary to sift, but make sure the baking soda and baking powder are well incorporated. In a smaller bowl, mix the buttermilk, eggs, vanilla, and melted butter. Make a well in the center of the dry ingredients, add the wet ingredients, and mix until just moistened. Add the apple and nuts at the end.

Grease a muffin tin and divide the batter to fill all of the cups evenly. Bake about 15 minutes, until a toothpick inserted in the center comes out clean. Let the muffins cool for 5 minutes, remove from the pan, and allow to cool on a wire rack for another 10 minutes. Serve warm with butter.

**VARIATIONS:** Use chopped firm pear such as Bosc. Substitute walnuts for hazelnuts. Add a teaspoon of orange or lemon zest. Try spelt flour instead of the rye.

---

### CINNAMON STREUSEL TOPPING

½ cup whole wheat flour

¼ cup dark brown sugar

½ teaspoon cinnamon

¼ cup butter, melted

In a small bowl, mix the flour, sugar, and cinnamon together. Pour the melted butter over the dry ingredients, and stir with a fork until the mixture is crumbly. Sprinkle the streusel topping on each muffin, lightly pressing the mixture into the batter. Bake as directed.

## OVERNIGHT OATCAKES

Oatcakes, also known as bannocks, are a traditional part of the Scottish diet. They were traditionally cooked on a griddle over the fire, but can be made in a heavy frying pan on the stove or baked in an oven. They are really more like what Americans call a cracker, but not salty nor quite as crispy as, say, your average wheat thin, though you can certainly sprinkle them with salt before baking, if you prefer. As they are, however, they are quite addictive and are delectable with butter and jam for tea, or with a dollop of apple butter alongside a cup of coffee, or topped with a bit of smoked salmon or extra-sharp cheddar with an aperitif in the evening.

**1½ cups steel-cut oats (Scottish oats)**

**¼ cup buttermilk, or yoghurt thinned to the consistency of buttermilk**

**¼ cup hot water**

**½ cup oat flour, whole wheat flour, or rye flour**

**¼ teaspoon salt**

**¼ teaspoon baking soda or baking powder**

**¼ cup melted butter**

**Flour for dusting**

Mix the oats, buttermilk, and hot water together in a large bowl. Cover and let the oats soak overnight or for about 8 hours while you go about your day.

Preheat the oven to 350°F.

Add the flour, salt, and baking soda or powder to the bowl, then pour the melted butter into the center. Stir well. You may need to add another tablespoon or so of buttermilk (or hot water). The dough will be stiff and a bit sticky.

Turn the dough out onto a work surface dusted with flour. Knead the dough several times until it comes together. Roll it out to ¼-inch thick. It may be helpful to spread a piece of waxed paper on your work surface, flatten the dough with your hands, then lay a second piece of waxed paper across the top, and roll over that. Using a round cookie cutter or the rim of a 3-inch diameter glass, cut the dough into round cakes. Re-roll the scraps, and continue cutting out circles until all the dough has been used. Place the cakes about ¼-inch apart on a baking sheet.

Alternatively, cut a piece of parchment paper to fit your baking sheet. Spread the parchment paper on a work surface, flatten the dough into a rough rectangle on the paper, then cover with a piece of waxed paper. Roll out the dough as thin as you can, then remove the waxed paper. Score with a pizza cutter to make rectangular crackers, and slide the parchment paper back onto the baking sheet.

Bake until golden brown, about 15 to 25 minutes, depending on thickness. You can flip them halfway through the cooking time for a crispier cracker. Remove from the oven and let cool on a wire rack.

You can also cook your oatcakes on a cast-iron griddle on the stove (or on the hearth over an open fire should you happen to be so equipped). Divide the dough into two balls, and roll out each to around ¼-inch thick. Place a plate, which is slightly smaller than the size of your griddle, over the flattened dough and cut around it to make a circular oatcake. Cut into quarters (called "farls") and place them on the lightly greased heated griddle. Cook over medium heat for about 3 minutes, until the edges curl slightly. Flip the cake and cook the other side. While the first oatcake is cooking, prepare the next.

**VARIATIONS:** Add 1 to 2 teaspoons of sugar, plus 1 teaspoon of anise seed to the dough for a sweeter cracker. Try experimenting with other spices, such as ground cardamom seeds.

## CHEF ZACHARY'S UNBELIEVABLE BUTTERMILK BISCUITS

Contributed by Stalford Farms in Tangent, Oregon.

My immediate reaction when I took a bite from the first trial batch of these biscuits was "Oh, my!" They are incredibly light and fluffy. The amount of butter involved is not insignificant, but they are a wonderful indulgence. Pair warm biscuits with a pot of fresh strawberry jam or raspberry jelly and a cup of tea and you will find that suddenly all is right with the world.

Makes 12 biscuits.

**2 cups whole wheat pastry flour — try Greenwillow Grains' soft white wheat pastry flour**

**2 teaspoons baking soda**

**1 teaspoon baking powder**

**2 Tablespoons brown sugar**

**2 teaspoons kosher salt**

**1 cup butter, grated — freeze or chill well for easier grating**

**1 cup buttermilk**

Preheat the oven to 400°F.

In a large mixing bowl, combine the flour, baking soda, baking powder, brown sugar, and salt. Mix very well, either by sifting or whisking. Add the grated butter into the flour mixture, then break up into smaller crumbs with your fingers or a pastry cutter. Make a well in the center of the flour and butter mix, and pour in the buttermilk. To make the biscuits light and fluffy, mix just until the dough is moist, then knead the dough gently until it holds together. You can do this in the bowl, or you can turn the dough out onto a floured surface.

Spoon 12 portions onto an ungreased baking sheet. If you prefer, you can pat the dough into a ¾-inch thick slab and cut out the biscuits with a round cookie cutter or the rim of a 3-inch diameter glass. The biscuits will spread considerably, so give them ample room. Bake until golden brown, about 15 to 20 minutes.

# GRAINS FOR DESSERT

Cookies, pie, and cake are perhaps the most common offerings when something sweet is called for. And they are usually made with white all-purpose flour, although they certainly don't need to be. There are many ways to incorporate whole grains into something tasty to end the meal! Puddings, for instance, were once in favor as the dessert of choice; in fact, the term "pudding" was once synonymous with dessert. Whole grains make great pudding! Creamy barley makes a pudding similar to rice pudding (page 190), and other whole grains lend themselves to pudding as well. *Dolce di Grano* (page 184), or sweet grains, is an Italian dessert made from whole farro and lots of rich spices and honey. Whole grains let you have your dessert and enhance your health at the same time. Wow!

### A SIMPLE FRUIT CRUMBLE

Crumbles are an easy way to start serving whole grains for dessert. Toss about 6 cups of sliced fruit (apples, pears, peaches, etc.) or whole berries with ¼ cup of sugar, a tablespoon of flour, and a teaspoon or so of lemon juice. Pile it in a deep pie pan or baking dish.

In the bowl of a food processor, combine 1 cup rolled oats, ¼ cup whole wheat flour, ¼ cup rye flour, ¼ cup brown sugar, and a pinch of salt. Buzz a few times, until the ingredients are well combined, and the oats are chopped up a bit.

Remove to a bowl and add 6 tablespoons of melted butter. With your hands, squeeze the mixture together until a crumbly mass forms. Scatter the topping over the fruit, and bake at 375°F, for 35 to 45 minutes, until the fruit is soft and the topping is golden brown. You can add spices such as cinnamon to the fruit or the topping as you wish.

## DOLCE DI GRANO

Inspired by a recipe from Stalford Farms.

*Dolce di Grano* is an Italian dish of wheat berries or farro laced with dried fruit, honey, and spices. Usually served for dessert, perhaps embellished with whipped cream, it can also be offered up with yoghurt, cream, or milk as a somewhat decadent breakfast.

Serves 6 to 8.

**1 cup farro (emmer) or wheat berries, sorted and soaked (see page 111)**

**1 fresh bay leaf**

**2 cups chopped fresh fruit, such as apples, cherries, plums**

**1 cup dried fruit, such as cranberries, tart cherries, chopped apricots**

**½ teaspoon cinnamon**

**¼ teaspoon mace or nutmeg**

**¼ cup honey**

**Pinch of salt**

**4 ounces very dark chocolate, chopped into ¼-inch pieces (optional)**

Drain the soaked farro or wheat berries. Place in a large pot with 2 cups of fresh water and the bay leaf. Bring to a boil, turn down to a simmer, cover, and cook for 30 minutes, until tender. Drain off any unabsorbed liquid, remove the bay leaf, and place the grain in a medium-size mixing bowl.

Add the fresh and dried fruit, spices, honey, and salt, and mix well. If using chocolate, add it as well.

Enjoy warm or at room temperature.

The fruit combinations can be varied infinitely, according to season, taste, and the contents of your larder.

## SPELT-HAZELNUT COOKIES

Contributed by Sue Hunton of Camas County Mill, who got the recipe from Dawn Woodward of Evelyn's Crackers in Ontario, Canada, at the 2013 Kneading Conference.

Makes about 45 cookies.

**2 sticks butter, softened**

**½ cup sugar**

**1 teaspoon vanilla extract**

**2 cups spelt flour**

**5 ounces hazelnuts, toasted and finely chopped**

Preheat the oven to 325°F.

Cream the butter with the sugar with a mixer until light and fluffy. Add the vanilla extract and the flour and mix well. Add the hazelnuts and mix again to combine. Chill the dough for 30 minutes.

Form the dough into two logs and slice into ¼-inch rounds. Place the slices on a baking sheet covered with parchment paper, and bake until lightly browned, about 18 to 20 minutes.

**VARIATION:** For a savory butter cookie, cut the amount of sugar in half and add ¼ teaspoon of salt and 1 tablespoon of finely chopped fresh rosemary.

## TEFF CHOCOLATE CHIP COOKIES—TWO WAYS

### VERSION I

In this recipe, contributed by Heidi Tunnell of Creswell, Oregon, maple syrup sweetens the cookies and peanut butter adds richness.

Makes 60 small cookies.

**3 cups teff flour**

**½ teaspoon salt**

**2 teaspoons baking soda**

**2 cups peanut butter**

**2 cups maple syrup**

**1 cup semi-sweet chocolate chips**

Preheat the oven to 350°F.

In a medium bowl, combine the teff flour, salt, and baking soda. In a larger bowl, combine the peanut butter and syrup, mixing well.

Gradually add the dry ingredients to the wet ingredients, mixing with a fork until just incorporated. Stir in the chocolate chips. Cover and chill the dough for several hours.

Drop dough by the rounded tablespoon two inches apart on two baking sheets lined with parchment paper. Flatten with a fork in the traditional manner of peanut butter cookies.

Bake until the bottoms are lightly browned and the cookies hold together when you lift them from the baking sheet, about 10 to 12 minutes.

**VARIATION:** Jennifer Burns Bright likes to substitute almond butter for the peanut butter.

## VERSION II

This recipe from the Willamette Farm and Food Coalition does not use nut butter.

Makes 2-dozen small cookies.

**1¼ cup teff flour**

**1 teaspoon baking soda**

**1 teaspoon salt**

**⅓ cup olive oil**

**1 cup sugar**

**1 teaspoon vanilla extract**

**1 egg**

**1 cup semi-sweet chocolate chips**

**½ cup walnuts (optional)**

Preheat the oven to 375°F.

In a small bowl, combine the teff flour, baking soda, and salt. In a large bowl, beat the oil, sugar, and vanilla until creamy, then add the egg and beat well. Gradually add the flour mixture to the wet ingredients. Stir in the chocolate chips and nuts (if using).

Drop by the rounded tablespoon onto an ungreased baking sheet. Bake for about 10 minutes, until the bottom is lightly browned. Cool on the baking sheet for a few minutes, then remove to a wire rack to cool completely.

## NOT YOUR NONNA'S BISCOTTI

In traditional Swedish foods, rye is often used in combination with orange and anise. As it happens, the combination works well with these not-so-traditional Italian cookies as well!

½ **cup butter, melted and then cooled**

¾ **cup sugar**

2 **eggs**

1 **teaspoon vanilla**

1 **teaspoon grated orange zest**

1 **Tablespoon anise seed**

2 **cups whole wheat flour — pastry flour, if you have it**

1 **cup dark rye flour**

3 **teaspoons baking powder**

½ **teaspoon salt**

½ **cup walnuts, chopped fairly finely**

Preheat the oven to 300°F.

In a large mixing bowl, cream the butter and sugar together well, then add the eggs and beat again. Mix in the vanilla, orange zest, and anise seed.

In a separate bowl, whisk together the flours, baking powder, and salt. Add the dry mixture to the wet, a bit at a time. Stir in the nuts at the last.

With damp hands, divide the dough in half and form 2 logs, ½-inch thick and about 2-inches wide. Place them on a greased baking sheet. Bake for 25 to 30 minutes, until cracks form on the surface of the logs and a toothpick inserted into the center comes out clean. Remove the baking sheet from the oven, and set it on a wire rack until the logs are cool to the touch. Keep the oven on, however.

When you can handle the logs, carefully move them to a cutting board. With a thin serrated knife (such as a bread knife) or your sharpest thin knife, carefully cut the logs on an angle into ½-inch thick slices. A decisive back and forth slicing motion seems to work best, and holding the sides of the slice you are cutting off helps to keep the cookie from crumbling. Set the slices upright (in other words, with an uncut side down) on a baking sheet. I usually use two baking sheets to accommodate all the slices without crowding them.

Bake the slices for another 25 to 30 minutes, until they feel firm and dry and look toasty. Keep the biscotti in a cookie tin or other closed container so they stay crisp.

**VARIATIONS:** Try hazelnuts or almonds instead of walnuts. Lemon zest can stand in for orange zest. Spelt flour could replace the rye.

### BISCOTTI OR CANTUCCINI?

*Biscotto* is Italian for "twice baked" and originally referred to many foods which were baked two times in order to dry them for easy storage over long periods of time—especially useful if you were a member of the Roman Legion. These days, we know biscotti as cookies. *Cantuccini* are a petite version of almond and anise flavored biscotti, and are often served in Tuscany with a glass of *vin santo* to dip the cookies in. Feel free to dip your biscotti into a cup of coffee or tea for an afternoon treat, if you are not packing them for an extended march.

## GOLDEN HULLESS BARLEY PUDDING WITH FRUIT COMPOTE

In this recipe, barley replaces rice for a stovetop pudding that is served with spicy stewed fruit.

Serves 4 to 6.

**1 cup golden hulless barley, sorted and soaked (see page 111)**

**2 cups milk—whole or low-fat, or substitute nut, soy, or rice milk**

**2-inch piece of vanilla bean**

**½ cup sugar**

Drain and rinse the soaked barley. Place in a large pot with a scant 3 cups of fresh water. Bring to a boil, turn down to a simmer, and cook, covered, for 30 to 45 minutes, until just tender and the liquid has been absorbed. This can be done ahead of time, and the cooked barley can be refrigerated until you are ready to make the pudding. (If you refrigerate the barley, however, bring it back up to room temperature or warm it slightly before you add it to the milk.)

Pour the milk into a 3-quart saucepan. Split the vanilla bean lengthwise and scrape out the tiny black seeds with the tip of a sharp knife. Add the seeds and the pod to the milk, along with the sugar. Slowly bring the milk to a boil over medium heat, then add the barley. Return to a boil, then turn down the heat to very low and simmer until the milk is almost all absorbed, about 45 to 60 minutes. Stir occasionally. When the pudding has finished cooking, remove the vanilla pod. Serve warm, and pass the Fruit Compote to be spooned over the top.

**VARIATION:** Try other whole grains instead of barley, such as farro or soft white winter wheat.

**NOTE:** Vanilla beans can usually be found in the bulk spice section. They are a bit dear, but a little goes a long way and the taste is very special. If you do not have a vanilla bean, substitute 1 teaspoon of vanilla extract. Taste the pudding at the end, and if you want a stronger vanilla flavor, add a bit more.

## FRUIT COMPOTE

**1 cup water**

**1 bag Earl Grey tea**

**¼ cup sugar**

**Small stick cinnamon**

**2 cloves**

**6 prune plums—frozen is OK—halved and pitted**

**1 cup chopped apple**

In a 1½-quart saucepan, bring the water to a boil, add the tea bag, and let steep for 3 minutes. Discard the tea bag, add the sugar, cinnamon stick, and cloves, and bring to a boil. Add the plums and apple, and lower the heat. Simmer for 5 minutes, until the plums are tender but not completely falling apart. Lift out the fruit with a slotted spoon, and transfer it to a serving dish. Reduce the liquid that is left in the saucepan by boiling it for 5 minutes, then remove the cinnamon stick and cloves, and pour the reduced liquid over the fruit.

**VARIATIONS:** Instead of Earl Grey tea, try steeping a bag or two of your favorite chai tea (no need to add the cinnamon stick or cloves). Substitute honey for the sugar. In the winter, use chopped dried apricots, prunes, and apples, along with some raisins.

## INDIAN PUDDING

Indian Pudding was a Thanksgiving tradition when I was growing up. My mother's recipe calls for yellow cornmeal, but I like it just as well if not more using polenta from locally grown heirloom corn varieties such as Abenaki Flint. The pudding was named by the early colonists, who were fond of a traditional English pudding called Hasty Pudding, made by boiling wheat flour in water or milk until it thickened into porridge. Since wheat flour was hard to obtain in those early days, the colonists substituted ground corn, which they called Indian flour.

**1 quart milk**

**1 cup polenta or cornmeal**

**¼ cup melted butter**

**⅔ cup molasses (not blackstrap)**

**⅛ teaspoon ground allspice**

**¼ teaspoon ground ginger**

**⅛ teaspoon ground nutmeg**

**½ teaspoon ground cinnamon**

**¼ teaspoon ground cloves**

**½ teaspoon salt**

**2 large eggs, beaten**

Preheat the oven to 350°F, and put a kettle of water on to boil.

In a large heavy-bottomed saucepan, heat the milk over medium heat, until bubbles form along the side of the pan but not to the point of boiling. Whisk in the polenta and cook at a gentle simmer, until thickened and the corn is soft, about 20 to 30 minutes, depending on whether you are using polenta or a more finely ground cornmeal.

Stir fairly constantly, as you would when making regular polenta. Alternatively, cook in a double boiler, which reduces but does not eliminate the need for stirring.

Remove from heat. In a small bowl, combine the butter, molasses, spices, and salt. Add the mixture to the saucepan. In the same bowl, beat the eggs. Add about ¼ cup of the hot pudding mixture to the bowl, then return the contents to the pot—this tempers the eggs and prevents them from scrambling.

Pour the pudding into a greased casserole dish. Place in a roasting pan filled with boiling water that reaches halfway up the side of the casserole dish. Bake for 1 to 2 hours, until the pudding is firm. Let the pudding set for 15 to 20 minutes, and serve warm with vanilla ice cream.

Should there be any pudding leftover, it can be reheated with a bit of milk for breakfast the next morning.

# FURTHER ADVENTURES WITH GRAINS

I had planned, at the outset, to include only recipes that were simple and could be made relatively quickly. But there are a few recipes that I really like, and I want to share them with you, even if you try them only once or twice. Offered up here for your delectation are two bread recipes and an introduction to nixtamalized corn. They are not difficult, but they do require a bit more of your time than the other recipes in the book. On the other hand, they are worth it!

### NIXTAMAL

Nixtamal is dried kernels of corn that have been soaked in pickling lime, also known as hydrated lime, calcium hydroxide, or Cal, to break down the outer pericarp that encloses the kernels. You can also use food-grade lye or clean wood ash to make nixtamal, but pickling lime is easy to use and readily available. Mrs. Wage's Pickling Lime can often be found near the canning goods in your grocery store.

**1 pound flint corn, such as Roy's Calais Flint or Abenaki Flint**

**2 Tablespoons pickling lime**

In a large enamel or stainless-steel pot, combine the corn kernels with the pickling lime. Add enough water to cover the corn by an inch or so. Bring to a bare simmer—don't let it boil!—and keep it at a simmer for an hour. Remove the pan from the heat, and let the kernels sit at room temperature overnight.

The next day, drain the corn and refresh under cold water. Rinse the kernels, rubbing them vigorously to slough off the pericarp. I find it helpful to place the corn in a bowl of fresh water in the sink and scoop up handfuls of the kernels, rubbing them briskly between my hands. Drain and refill the bowl as it becomes clouded with the bits of pericarp, and repeat until the water stays fairly clear and most of the kernels are free of their skin. Some bits of the pericarp will remain on the kernels, particularly with dark-colored kernels (purple especially), but don't fret too much, the corn is still edible and will still taste good.

You now have nixtamal, or alkalinized corn.

## HOMINY

To make hominy, place the nixtamal in a soup pot with enough fresh water to cover by two inches. Bring to a boil and then reduce to a simmer. Cook until the kernels are tender and the majority have split open. The amount of time this takes varies, depending on the type of corn you are using—somewhere between one and three hours. Alternatively, you can use a slow cooker and let it cook all day. The corn absorbs a lot of water, however, so check the pot regularly and add more liquid as needed. The hominy is now ready to use in a soup or stew. One pound of corn makes a lot of hominy, so freeze the extra as you would cooked beans.

If you don't have time to make your own nixtamal but want to experiment with posole and homemade tortillas, you can order dried nixtamal from Rancho Gordo or find it in Mexican food markets.

### NEED TO NIXTAMALIZE?

Long ago, people in Central America developed the technique of soaking maize (an ancient form of corn) in water mixed with ashes from their wood fires. The maize's tough outer hull was loosened, and the alkali in the ashes enhanced the corn's protein content. Some millennia later, corn was adopted as a staple food by Europeans and Africans, but the knowledge of nixtamal was not transmitted. In many areas, such as the rural American south, this lead to widespread malnourishment and pellagra, a painful and sometimes fatal disorder caused by a vitamin B3 deficiency.

## HOMINY WITH CHILE AND TOMATO BRAISED MEAT

Linda Colwell, a French-trained chef living and working in Portland, contributed this recipe for pairing hominy with a stew of brined tongue braised in a rich chile sauce. If you are not inclined to cook tongue, braised pork shoulder is a good substitute.

### HOMINY

**1 pound of Roy's Calais Flint or Abenaki Flint corn**

**2 Tablespoons pickling lime**

Follow the Hominy recipe on page 195.

### BRAISED TONGUE

**NOTE:** The tongue first needs to be brined for 5 days.

**1 beef tongue**

**4 quarts water**

**3 cups Morton's kosher salt**

**2 cups brown sugar**

**2 bay leaves**

**10 crushed juniper berries**

**10 crushed peppercorns**

**1 cinnamon stick**

**1 Tablespoon mustard seeds**

In a stainless-steel soup pot, bring the water, salt, sugar, bay leaves, and spices to a boil, then let cool overnight in the refrigerator. Thoroughly rinse the tongue and place it and the brine in a glass or plastic container large enough for the tongue to fit completely submerged. Refrigerate for 5 days.

Remove the tongue from the brine, rinse under cold water, and place it in a pot. Cover the tongue with fresh water and simmer, until it is tender, about 2 hours.

Preheat the oven to 250°F. Remove the tongue from the poaching liquid, and when cool, peel off the rough skin. Place the tongue in a Dutch oven, add the Chile and Tomato Sauce (see below), and braise in the oven for 2 hours.

When the meat is done, remove it to a platter. Add the hominy to the pot with the Chile and Tomato Sauce. Warm the hominy over medium-low heat, adding additional stock or water to the sauce as needed. Slice the meat, and add it to back to the pot of hominy and sauce. Serve with a garnish of chopped cilantro.

## CHILE AND TOMATO SAUCE

**4 each: dried Ancho chiles, dried pasilla chiles, dried guajillo chiles**

**3 cups boiling water**

**1 quart of tomato sauce**

Cut open the chiles with a pair of scissors, remove the seeds and stems, and break the chiles into smaller pieces. Lightly toast the chiles in a cast-iron skillet, then transfer to a bowl, cover with boiling water, and soak for 20 minutes. When soft, purée the chiles into a smooth paste and mix thoroughly with the tomato sauce.

## AN ALTERNATIVE: BRAISED PORK SHOULDER

**3-pound (approximately) pork shoulder**

Season the meat with salt and pepper. In a Dutch oven, heat a few tablespoons of peanut oil or olive oil. Brown the meat on all sides over medium-high heat. Remove the meat and set aside. Deglaze the pot by adding a bit of broth or wine and scraping off any pieces of meat that are stuck to the pan. Add the Chile and Tomato Sauce and return the meat to the pot. Cover and place the pot on the middle rack of a 375°F oven. Cook for one hour. Turn the meat over and cook for another hour. Check to see if the meat is done—it should offer little or no resistance to a knife or skewer. If not yet tender, cook further, turning every 30 minutes. The total cooking time might be as long as 3½ hours, depending on the size and cut of the meat.

## HOMEMADE TORTILLAS

Krista Rome, of the Backyard Bean and Grain Project, contributed these instructions for homemade tortillas. Krista prefers to use dent corn in her tortillas, as it contains a higher percentage of soft starch, making it easier to grind. Flint corn works as well, and is very tasty, but produces a coarser masa (tortilla dough). Krista uses a slightly different method of nixtamalizing the corn.

**2 cups dent corn kernels such as Mandan Bride, or flint corn such as Abenaki Flint or Roy's Calais Flint**

**2 Tablespoons pickling lime**

**6 cups water**

**Cooking oil**

You will also need:

**Masa (corn) grinder or food processor**

**Tortilla press or other pressing method**

Add the pickling lime to the water and slowly heat until dissolved. Add the corn kernels and continue heating on medium to low heat, stirring occasionally. It's best to heat very slowly, taking about 30 minutes to come to a simmer.

Simmer for 5 to 10 minutes, then let the corn sit for the day or overnight.

Rinse the kernels thoroughly in a bowl, with several changes of water, rubbing briskly to remove all of the lime and pericarp.

Drain the corn, then grind in small batches, using the grinder attachment to a stand mixer, a food processor, or better yet, a corn grinder such as a Corona, Estrella, or Victoria (available in Mexican food stores and online). Some food processors may not grind the corn fine enough, particularly if you are using flint corn. If this is the case, you can add some store-bought masa flour to help it bind together in the next step. (Bob's Red Mill produces a masa flour that does not contain GMO corn.)

Transfer the ground corn to a large bowl. Add just enough water —a few tablespoons to ¼ cup—to knead into a dough. The dough should hold together and not be overly sticky.

Make golfball-size balls and cover them with a damp tea towel so they don't dry out. Press the masa balls in a tortilla press. It is helpful to line the press with a cut-open and oiled plastic bag. If you do not have a press, you can roll the tortillas with a rolling pin, using a piece of waxed paper on each side of the masa to keep it from sticking.

Heat a dry cast-iron skillet on medium heat. Fry the tortillas on both sides, until just starting to turn golden brown.

Wet masa dough will keep in the refrigerator for several days.

### BASIC SALSA

A bright, fairly mild salsa fresca. The fresh tomatoes, lime, and cilantro work together to really make your mouth come alive.

**2 to 3 large tomatoes or 5 to 6 Roma tomatoes, chopped**

**½ onion—red, white, or yellow—minced**

**½ cup chopped cilantro**

**1 large clove garlic, minced**

**Juice of 1 lime**

**Salt to taste**

In a medium bowl, toss all of the ingredients together. Adjust the seasonings to suit your taste. The tomatoes will release more juice the longer the salsa sits. Best at room temperature.

**VARIATIONS:** Add chopped, seeded jalapeño or Serrano pepper, chunks of avocado, or minced sweet pepper. Combine different varieties and colors of tomatoes—yellow cherry tomatoes, deep red slicing tomatoes, colorful heirloom tomatoes.

## POSOLE

Posole is a traditional Mexican dish from the Pacific Coast region of Jalisco. At its most basic, it is a thick soup that's usually made with pork, but always features hominy, garlic, onion, chiles, cilantro, and broth. Like so many traditional dishes, there are hundreds of variations. Here are two.

### JENNIFER'S SORT-OF POSOLE

**Whole pork shoulder**

**1 onion**

**A few cloves garlic, peeled**

**1 bay leaf**

**6 to 8 cups of stock**

**2 cups of Hominy (see page 195)**

**1 cup finely chopped, roasted pasilla chiles**

**Salsa or chopped fresh tomatoes**

**Chopped cilantro**

Place the pork shoulder in a stock pot with the onion, garlic, bay leaf, and enough water to cover by several inches. Bring to a boil, then reduce the heat, and simmer for a few hours. When it is tender, shred the meat—you can reserve some for tacos, and use the rest and the cooking liquid for the posole.

In a soup pot, combine the stock with 2 cups of shredded pork, the hominy, and the pasilla chiles. Bring to a boil, reduce to a simmer, and cook for 30 minutes, until the ingredients are heated through. Just before serving, add the salsa or fresh tomatoes. Serve with chopped cilantro.

## POSOLE SOUP WITH BEANS

Here is another version of posole, meat optional.

**3 roasted chiles such as Anaheim or Poblano, fresh or frozen**

**Vegetable oil**

**1 small onion, chopped**

**2 cloves garlic, minced**

**1 teaspoon oregano**

**4 cups rich chicken or vegetable broth**

**1 cup chopped fresh tomatoes, or equivalent frozen**

**1 to 2 cups Hominy (see page 195)**

**1 to 2 cups cooked pinto-type beans such as Eye of the Tiger or Rio Zape (see page 29)**

**1 cup cooked shredded chicken or pork (optional)**

**Salt and pepper**

**Fresh lime**

**Fresh cilantro**

Slit the chiles open and remove the seeds. Place the chiles in a food processor and purée until smooth.

In a large soup pot, heat the oil, then add the onion and garlic and sauté until soft. Add the oregano, chile purée, broth, and tomatoes. Bring to a boil and reduce to a simmer. Add the hominy and beans and simmer for 20 minutes, until the tomatoes have broken down and the flavors are well acquainted. Add the meat (if using) and simmer until warm. Season to taste with salt and pepper.

Serve with lots of fresh lime and chopped cilantro, thinly sliced cabbage and radishes, and minced onion.

## FARMOR'S LIMPA

Limpa is a Swedish rye bread that I make every year at Christmas, but really it could be made at any time of year. The original recipe from my grandmother called for a combination of white flour and rye flour, but I enjoy it with whole wheat flour mixed with rye flour. It is a very dense, almost cake-like bread, and when toasted and spread with as much butter as your conscience will allow, it is divine.

**2 packages dry yeast**

**1½ cups warm water (about 100°F)**

**¼ cup molasses**

**¼ cup sugar**

**1 Tablespoon salt**

**1 teaspoon <u>each</u>: fennel seed, anise seed, and cardamom seed, pulverized together in a spice grinder or with a mortar and pestle**

**Grated rind of 2 oranges**

**2 Tablespoons soft butter**

**2½ cups rye flour**

**2½ cups whole wheat flour**

In a large mixing bowl, sprinkle the yeast and a pinch of sugar over the warm water, and stir until it is dissolved. Set in a warm place for 5 to 10 minutes to proof the yeast.

When the surface is nice and bubbly, add the molasses, sugar, salt, spices, orange rind, and butter. Stir in the rye flour, then when thoroughly blended, mix in the whole wheat flour, a cup at a time.

When the dough is too stiff to work in the bowl, turn it out onto a counter or breadboard dusted with flour and knead in the remaining flour. Continue to knead until the dough is satiny, about 10 minutes.

Place the dough in an oiled bowl, cover with plastic wrap or a tea towel, set in a warm place, and let rise until doubled, about 1½ to 2 hours.

Punch down and let rise again, until doubled, about 1 hour.

Punch down yet again, and divide the dough in two. Shape each half into a round loaf, then place both loaves on an oiled baking sheet. Cover with a tea towel and let rise until doubled, about an hour.

Preheat the oven to 350°F.

Bake for 35 minutes. When the loaves come out of the oven, brush the tops with melted butter and let cool on a wire rack.

## SOURDOUGH RYE STARTER

I love rye bread. Many people think they don't because really they don't like the taste of caraway seeds, which so often are added to rye bread. Rye flour itself is rich and sort of nutty, and it is fantastic for making sourdough. As an added benefit, when you make bread using only rye flour, there is no need to knead—or rather, there is no point in kneading, really, because rye bread rises by virtue of polysaccharide compounds called "pentosans" which enable the dough to hold the gas—which causes the dough to rise.

To start, you need a sourdough starter. You have two options here. You can go online and purchase a sourdough starter. Alternatively, you can start your own!

In a jar or a bowl, mix together a couple of tablespoons of non-chlorinated water and a couple of tablespoons of rye flour. Stir it well. I like to drop an unwashed grape, blueberry, or small plum into the mixture. These fruits have wild yeast on their skin—that's what gives them the sort of dusty film you see when you get them straight, unwashed, from the tree or bush. Use organic fruit, but don't wash it.

Cover the jar or bowl with cheesecloth, so that flies are kept out but air can circulate. Keep it in a warm place—70 to 80°F is great, but yeast can grow at somewhat lower temperatures given enough time. Stir your batter as frequently as you can—this stimulates the yeast and gets things going faster.

After 48 hours, add another tablespoon of flour and another tablespoon of water. Blend well and let it sit another 24 hours, stirring frequently.

Repeat this routine for three or four days. You should begin to see tiny bubbles coming to the surface of the batter. It's *aliiive*! If you don't find any bubbles forming after three or four days, find a warmer spot or add a pinch of packaged yeast or a commercial sourdough starter. If at any time, the batter starts to smell wrong (it should have a pleasant sour smell, not a putrid one) or starts to grow mold, toss it out and start over.

Once you have yeast activity established, take out the fruit and add a few tablespoons each of flour and water every day for three or four days, and continue to stir often. You are now feeding your yeast herd and encouraging it to go forth and multiply. Add a few more tablespoons of water if the batter starts to get very thick. Keep your starter in a covered bowl or jar on the counter, or in the refrigerator if you don't bake very often.

You now have an established sourdough starter, and you can start cooking with it. Following is the recipe that I use to make one loaf of plain sourdough rye. You can certainly double it if bread is gobbled up faster at your house than at mine.

Each time you bake, you need to replenish your starter by replacing the water and flour you remove. If you use 1 cup of starter in your recipe, add a cup of flour and a cup of water.

In our house, the starter is known as The Mother (from the Italian *lievito madre*, or "living mother"). The Mother gets fed every Saturday, the day we usually start a new loaf of bread. If we aren't going to bake, we feed The Mother just a quarter cup of flour and water, so she doesn't get too big for her bowl.

There is a great deal of good literature on sourdough cultures and baking with them. Visit your library or your bookstore, or hop on the internet to find recipes and do some research to supplement the process that I have described. It's wild!

## SOURDOUGH RYE BREAD

**1 cup Sourdough Rye Starter (see page 204)**

**1½ cups water**

**4 cups rye flour, divided**

**½ teaspoon salt**

If you keep your starter in the refrigerator, take it out the night before you start your loaf, so it will be warm and the yeast will be active.

In the morning, mix the starter with 2 cups of the rye flour and the water. Stir well, then let it sit in a warm place, covered with cheesecloth, for 8 to 24 hours. Stir occasionally. This is the first sour.

That evening, before you go to bed, add the remaining 2 cups of rye flour and the salt to the mixture. Stir well, cover, and let the bowl sit in a warm place overnight. This is the second sour.

In the morning, your dough will have risen noticeably. Gently ease it out of the bowl and form it into a round loaf. Rye dough is *very* sticky! Be patient with it. A plastic dough scraper will come in handy here. Moistening your hands also helps. Your loaf now needs to rise for another hour. I bake my loaf on a preheated pizza stone, so I let the loaf rise on a pizza peel that has been well dusted with oat bran or cornmeal. Alternatively, grease a baking sheet (or use parchment paper), and let the loaf rise on that.

When your loaf is ready to bake, preheat the oven to 350°F. Bake for 1½ hours or more, until the loaf sounds hollow when you tap the bottom. Cool on a wire rack and try to let it sit for at least 15 minutes before you slice it.

Sourdough rye stays moist far longer than most yeasted breads, and I think it is actually better after a few days. The crust will become a bit hard, so you will want to use a good sharp serrated bread knife. It is excellent cut into thin slices, toasted, and adorned with soft goat cheese (or butter) or sharp cheddar (or butter) or any number of other toppings (or butter).

Enjoy!

# NUTS AND SEEDS

Back in the Dark Ages, when I was a kid, nuts came in their shells. Or at least that is how they came to my house. Generally, they arrived at Thanksgiving time and had a significant presence through the holidays. During cocktail hour, my father would frequent the bowl of walnuts, almonds, Brazil nuts, and filberts, wielding his nutcracker and handing out the odd shelled nut to any child who happened to be passing by at the right moment.

More important, however, or at least to me, was the role that nuts played in Christmas cookies. Since bulk bins full of shelled almonds and filberts and walnuts had yet to appear in the grocery store, if we wanted Christmas cookies, we had to crack those nuts. As soon as we were old enough to handle a nutcracker, we were seated in a chair next to the old butcher-block table, a bowl of nuts on our lap, an empty bowl next to us on the table, and a bag for the shells at our feet. Swedish spritz cookies and moon cookies require, in addition to vast quantities of butter, a lot of almonds, which had to be extracted from their shells and then doused with hot water so their skins would slip off. This was serious labor — but well worth the effort!

Nowadays, bags of shelled nuts of all varieties are easy to come by, and jars full of almonds and filberts and walnuts have long been a staple at our house. It is my experience, however, that a freshly shelled nut has far more flavor, and I suspect more nutrition, than any of the nutmeats that come prepackaged and ready for munching. The shell of the nut has been well designed for keeping the meat inside fresh, whereas shelled nuts should really be stored in the freezer to ward off rancidity.

Of late, a bowl filled with locally grown, unshelled filberts and walnuts has taken up residence in my house each year around Thanksgiving. My kids, my spouse, and visitors with free hands are employed in cracking the nuts when I want a quantity of filberts to toast or walnuts for making biscotti. It is not an onerous task, and it pulls the household together into the making of our food. We are in the habit now of bringing the bowl of nuts to join us at the table for dessert. Paired with a bit of fruit or cheese, they make a lovely, convivial closing to the meal. We savor each hand-shelled nut far more than those we toss back by the handful, pre-shelled, from a bag.

Nutritionally speaking, nuts are a great deal. A plant-based protein, they also contain lots of fiber and various combinations of vitamins, minerals, and antioxidants. Nuts are very high in the type of fats that are good for us—the mono- and polyunsaturated kinds. The combination of fat, fiber, and protein makes nuts a great addition to a meal or a good snack, at least in small quantities.

Seeds are another excellent source of locally grown protein. Some of the "grains" in the grain section, such as millet and buckwheat, are in fact seeds, but we treat them as grains. I suppose you can argue that all nuts are seeds, just as all grains are seeds, but there are some seeds that don't lend themselves to being treated as a grain, nor do they act like a nut. I'm thinking of sunflower seeds, sesame seeds, and flax seeds. Like nuts they contain a good deal of oil, and with the proper equipment can be processed into cooking oil.

Farmers markets often sell bags of locally grown nuts in the shell. They have already been dried and are easy to store in the back of the pantry or an unused closet. Alternatively, you can gather your own nuts!

# HARVESTING NUTS

**Walnuts.** English walnut trees line the streets of many towns, but the walnuts themselves are often left on the sidewalk or swept to the gutter. There is no reason they can't be eaten! It is polite to ask homeowners for permission, which is generally granted as it means less cleanup for them. Once you have been given the OK, first remove the existing fallen nuts (as you can't be sure how long they have been lying around). Then return to the tree every day or so, and pick up the nuts that have fallen.

Walnuts are encased in a very stout, green outer coat that needs to be removed within a day or two after the nut falls to the ground. If the husk is left on longer, its bitterness will leach through the shell and into the walnut, rendering it inedible. Gloves are advisable, as this can be a messy procedure. The nuts then need to be dried in their shells. You can spread them out in a shallow boxtop or on a baking sheet, or hang them in a mesh bag (such as an onion bag), in a warm place, where there is good air circulation. After a few weeks, crack one open and taste it. Green walnuts will be slightly bitter (although interestingly, the Italians use green walnuts to make their walnut liqueur). A completely dried walnut will have a bit of crunch to it and taste... well, like a walnut.

**Hazelnuts.** Hazelnuts (or filberts) are harvested somewhat differently. Hazelnut orchards are wonderful, shady places, and the trees are much more accessible than mature walnut trees. The earliest nuts to drop from the tree and out of their husks tend to have worms in them, so avoid those. Nuts that fall with their husks still attached are good if the hazelnut can be easily flicked out. You can also pick clusters of hazelnuts off the tree; if they come off easily, they are ripe, and if the nut wiggles free easily, it is most likely worm-free. Again, as with walnuts, hazelnuts need to be spread out or hung in a mesh bag to dry in a warm place. After a few weeks of air drying, the color of the shell will deepen, and the nut inside will lose its green taste and will be a bit crunchy. Stored with adequate air circulation, hazelnuts will last the winter and into early spring.

## COOKING WITH NUTS AND SEEDS

Nuts and seeds can be added to a variety of recipes to boost nutrition and flavor. Finely ground nuts can thicken stews and soups, as in, for instance, Winter Squash Stew with Purple Barley (page 172). Similarly, a spoonful of nut butter can be added to your porridge or morning smoothie for a bit of extra richness and protein. Toasted nuts and seeds are fantastic in salads of all kinds and are great additions to pilaf and pasta. I like to toast sesame seeds and flax seeds and mix them with shredded toasted nori (seaweed) for a Sort-of Furikake —the Japanese sprinkle seasoning traditionally scattered on a bowl of rice (page 231). Enhance butter by blending it with finely chopped, toasted nuts, much as you would make herb butter; then for a real treat, add a dab to a bowl of creamy or bisque soup. Lightly steamed green beans are excellent when tossed with toasted hazelnuts or walnuts, a bit of olive oil, salt, and strips of sweet red pepper.

### TOASTING NUTS AND SEEDS

Toasting nuts and seeds makes them more easily digestible, although there is evidence that the nutrient profile is somewhat decreased. Toasting also deepens the nuts' flavor. Nuts can be toasted in a 300 to 325°F oven or in a dry skillet on the stovetop, for about 10 minutes, depending on the size of the nut.

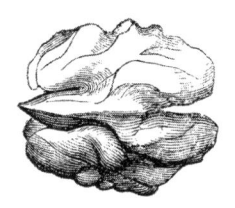

# SPROUTING NUTS

As is the case with beans and grains, nuts contain phytic acid. Sprouting nuts breaks down the phytic acid making the nuts' nutrients more available to us and increasing digestibility. Sprouted nuts and seeds are also higher in protein and lower in carbohydrates, as the sprouting process uses some of the stored carbohydrates.

Place 4 cups of nuts (walnuts, hazelnuts, almonds) in a glass jar or bowl with 2 to 3 teaspoons of sea salt dissolved in enough water to cover the nuts completely. Cover with a tea towel or a piece of cheesecloth. Keep the container out of direct sunlight and give the nuts a good soak, somewhere between 7 to 12 hours. Don't soak them longer than 12 hours, or they will rot instead of sprout. Overnight is a good length of time.

Next, drain the nuts completely. Nuts will not develop a shoot as beans and grains do, rather, they will swell and may produce a bulge at one end.

Once your nuts are soaked, they need to be dehydrated so they don't mold. A food dehydrator works well, or you can dry them in your oven if it can be set at a very low temperature (150°F). Dehydrate for 12 to 24 hours, until completely dry and crisp.

# BAKED GOODS AND DESSERTS

Nuts and seeds are a healthy, tasty addition to all sorts of baked goods, both sweet and savory. Ground finely, nut meal can replace part or all of the flour in many cookies and crackers. Folded into breads, nuts and seeds boost flavor as well as add protein. Try adding different combinations of nuts and seeds into some of your favorite recipes!

## DRIED FRUIT AND NUT CROSTINI

Whole grain, unsweetened, quick bread batter is garnished with toasted nuts, seeds, and dried fruit. After freezing, the loaf is easily sliced and baked again, as you would biscotti. Delicious served with a soft goat cheese.

¼ cup toasted pumpkin seeds

¼ cup flax seeds

¼ cup chopped hazelnuts

¼ cup dried cranberries

¼ cup chopped dried figs

½ Tablespoon minced fresh rosemary or 1 teaspoon fennel seeds

½ teaspoon lemon zest (with rosemary) or orange zest (with fennel)

1 cup whole wheat flour, or substitute half rye, spelt, or other similar flour

1 teaspoon baking soda

¼ teaspoon salt

1 cup buttermilk

Preheat the oven to 350°F.

In a small bowl, combine the seeds, nuts, dried fruit, and rosemary and lemon zest, or fennel seeds and orange lemon zest.

Whisk the flour, baking soda, and salt together in a large bowl. With a few quick strokes, stir in the buttermilk. Add the seed-nut-fruit mixture and stir until blended.

Grease an 8 x 4-inch loaf pan (or two mini-pans), and pour in the batter. Bake for 25 minutes, until golden, firm to the touch, and the loaf starts to pull away from the sides of the pan.

Remove the loaf from the pan and cool on a wire rack. When cool, wrap the loaf tightly and put it in the freezer for a few hours.

When the loaf is partially frozen, slice very thin (¼ inch) and place the slices on an ungreased baking sheet. Bake at 300°F, for 15 minutes, then flip and bake another 15 minutes, until the crostini are toasted and crisp.

Cool on a wire rack and store in an airtight container.

This recipe can easily be doubled; the second unsliced loaf can be frozen for up to two months.

**VARIATIONS:** Substitute walnuts for the hazelnuts. Sprinkle the top of the loaf with coarse salt before baking.

## HAZELNUT CRACKERS

Nut meal replaces some of the flour in these rich, whole wheat crackers.

Makes 30 or so crackers.

**1 cup hazelnuts**

**½ cup whole wheat flour, or substitute another whole grain flour such as spelt or rye**

**½ teaspoon salt**

**3 Tablespoons olive oil**

**3 to 4 Tablespoons cold water**

Toast the hazelnuts in a low oven or in a dry cast-iron skillet, until the skins start to break but the nuts are still cream-colored inside. Cool to the touch. You can rub the skins off if you like, but I leave them on as they add to the rich brown color of the crackers.

Preheat the oven to 350°F.

Place the hazelnuts, flour, and salt in a food processor and buzz until the texture resembles that of cornmeal. With the processor running, slowly add the olive oil through the feeder tube. Add the water, a bit at a time, until the mixture starts to come together and looks like a dough. You may need more or less water. If you don't have a food processor, grind the nuts in a blender, then combine them with the remainder of the ingredients in a mixing bowl.

Let the dough rest a few minutes while you cut a piece of parchment paper to fit a rimmed baking sheet. Place the trimmed parchment paper on a cutting board.

Remove the dough to the parchment paper and, with your hands, flatten it to a rough rectangle. Cover the dough with a piece of waxed paper, and roll it out to ¼-inch or less. If some of the dough pushes out past the parchment paper, use a knife to cut off the excess, and use it to fill in whatever corner could use some filling in. The goal is to make a very thin sheet of dough that more or less covers the entire parchment paper.

> **GO CRACKERS!**
>
> You can make crackers without nuts, of course. For a savory cracker, try mixing ¾ cup of soft white wheat flour with ¾ cup of other whole grain flour, and add the salt, olive oil, and water as called for in the recipe. Before baking, dust the top with grated Parmesan cheese, coarse salt, sesame or poppy seeds, or your favorite spice mix.
>
> If you have a pasta machine, you can use it to make your cracker dough *very* thin. Divide the dough into small pieces, and put each through the rollers as you would pasta dough, getting down to a number 4 setting.
>
> Crackers can be baked on a pre-heated pizza stone for extra crispiness. After you roll out the dough, transfer it to a pizza peel that has been dusted with cornmeal or flour. Prick the dough with a fork and slide it onto the stone. You can score the dough first or break your crackers into irregular pieces after they have baked.

With a pizza cutter, cut the dough into 2- or 3-inch squares or rectangles or whatever shape suits your fancy. Prick the crackers with a fork. Slide the parchment paper with the dough onto the baking sheet. Bake for 12 to 15 minutes, until the crackers feel firm and are toasty brown. Watch them carefully—they burn easily!

Cool the crackers on a wire rack. In theory, they will keep for a week or two in an airtight container, but in all likelihood, they will be gone before then.

## FARMOR'S HAZELNUT COOKIES

This is a traditional Christmas cookie in my family, although here I have reduced the amount of sugar so that the flavor of the hazelnuts really shines. The nuts are ground to a fine meal, which replaces flour completely.

Makes about 30 cookies.

**1½ cups hazelnuts**

**2 eggs**

**½ cup sugar**

**Pinch of salt**

**1 teaspoon vanilla**

Preheat the oven to 325°F.

Grind the hazelnuts in a food processor or blender until finely ground but not to the point of hazelnut butter. Remove to a mixing bowl.

Cream the eggs with the sugar, salt, and vanilla with a mixer, and add to the ground hazelnuts.

On a baking sheet covered with parchment paper, place teaspoonfuls of the cookie dough about one inch apart. Bake for 15 minutes, until the cookies are light brown around the edges. They will seem underdone. Watch the cookies carefully, as they can burn in a snap.

Remove the cookies to a wire rack to cool.

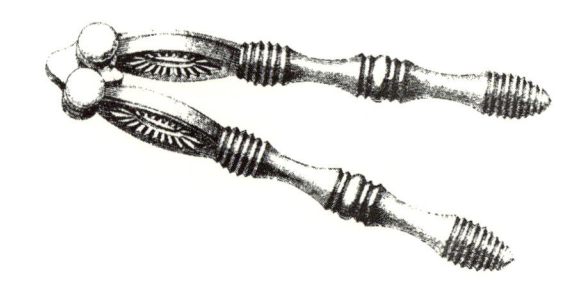

## CLAUDIA'S HAZELNUT COOKIES WITH CHOCOLATE

Makes about 3-dozen cookies.

**1½ cups whole wheat pastry flour**

**Pinch salt**

**1 teaspoon baking powder**

**2 sticks butter, room temperature**

**1 egg, beaten**

**1 teaspoon vanilla**

**¾ cup sugar**

**1½ cups finely ground hazelnuts**

**Dark chocolate buttons**

Preheat the oven to 350°F.

In a small bowl, whisk together the flour, salt, and baking powder.

In a stand mixer or using a hand-held mixer, cream the butter, egg, vanilla, and sugar. Mix in the hazelnuts and the dry mixture. This will form a stiff dough—you may have to mix it by hand if it is too much for your mixer.

Form the dough into 1-inch balls, and place them one inch apart on a baking sheet. Press a chocolate button in the center of each. Bake until golden brown, about 20 to 25 minutes.

**VARIATIONS:** The dough can also be chilled, rolled out, and cut into shapes with cookie cutters. Or, instead of topping your cookie with a chocolate button, press the balls down with a fork in the manner of peanut butter cookies.

## PANFORTE

Adapted from a recipe by Lisa Skopil, a pastry chef in Eugene, Oregon.

*Panforte* means "strong bread" in Italian and is a mixture of dried fruits and nuts mixed with honey and sugar. Many traditional recipes call for the addition of cocoa, but I like the spices and honey to shine.

**1 cup coarsely chopped, toasted hazelnuts**

**1 cup coarsely chopped, toasted almonds**

**2 cups chopped dried fruit—I generally use ½ cup each of dates, figs, cranberries, and apricots**

**1 teaspoon grated lemon zest**

**½ cup flour**

**1 teaspoon cinnamon**

**¼ teaspoon ground coriander**

**¼ teaspoon ground cloves**

**¼ teaspoon nutmeg**

**Pinch white pepper**

**¾ cup honey**

**¾ cup white sugar**

**2 Tablespoons butter**

Preheat the oven to 300°F.

Mix the nuts, dried fruit, lemon zest, flour, and spices in a large mixing bowl and set aside.

Butter a 9-inch springform pan. Line the bottom and sides of the pan with parchment paper, then butter the paper. If you don't have a springform pan, use an 8 x 8-inch glass baking dish and bring the edges of the parchment paper up over the sides so you can lift out the baked panforte.

In a heavy-bottomed saucepan, mix the honey, sugar, and butter over low heat, stirring constantly, until the sugar melts into the honey and the mixture is foamy and registers 242 to 248°F on a candy thermometer. Immediately pour the syrup onto the nut mixture and stir quickly until thoroughly blended. Transfer the batter to the springform pan (or baking dish) and smooth the top with a spatula. The batter will become stiff and sticky, so you need to work fast.

Bake the panforte for 30 to 40 minutes. It will not seem very firm to the touch, but will harden as it cools. Cool on a wire rack until the cake is firm to the touch. Remove the side of the pan and invert the cake onto a sheet of waxed paper. Peel off the parchment paper. Wrap in plastic wrap and store at room temperature. Panforte is very rich, so serve small slices.

**VARIATIONS:** Substitute other dried fruits, such as sour cherries, mangoes, or apples. Candied ginger (just a bit) gives a nice zing. Or add a bit of candied orange peel if you are fond of that flavor.

## SUGAR PLUMS

Sugar plums are more than just visions dancing in the heads of peacefully sleeping children! Before Christmas was drenched in layers of super-sweet cookies and cakes and candies, dried fruits and nuts were a holiday treat. Sugar plums were one of those holiday foods. This version is eminently suitable for adaptation to incorporate your tastes and whatever dried fruits and nuts you have on hand. And you don't have to confine the making of these treats to the Yuletide!

**1 cup hazelnuts**

**1 Tablespoon lemon zest**

**1 teaspoon cinnamon**

**¼ teaspoon each: ground coriander, cloves, and nutmeg**

**1 cup chopped dried figs**

**½ cup each: chopped dried apricots and chopped dried apples**

**¼ cup chopped dates**

**¼ cup chopped prunes**

**1 Tablespoon honey**

**Unsweetened toasted coconut (optional)**

Preheat the oven to 250°F.

Toast the hazelnuts in the oven for 10 minutes. Allow to cool, then place in a food processor with the lemon zest and the spices and process briefly. Add the dried fruits and the honey and process until a fairly smooth dough develops.

Roll the dough into ½- to 1-inch balls. If desired, roll the balls in coconut. Store in a closed container with sheets of waxed paper between layers.

**VARIATIONS:** Try walnuts or almonds instead of hazelnuts, or use a combination. Vary the spices—try ground cardamom, or add some allspice. Orange zest can replace the lemon zest. A bit of chopped very dark chocolate might be a nice addition.

# NUTTY NIBBLES AND SEEDY BARS

Seasoned nuts have been a regular offering at cocktail parties for as long as anyone can remember. They are so easy to make and much less expensive than a bag or a can purchased at the grocery store!

## SPICY ROSEMARY HAZELNUTS WITH ORANGE ZEST

Contributed by Jennifer Burns Bright.

Makes enough for a party.

**4 cups hazelnuts**

**1 cup dark brown sugar**

**⅓ cup finely chopped fresh rosemary, do not use dried**

**1 Tablespoon coarse kosher salt**

**1 teaspoon finely chopped fresh orange zest**

**Several healthy dashes of hot sauce, or a splash of vinegar**

Preheat the oven to 350°F.

Toast the hazelnuts in the oven for 10 minutes. It is not necessary to rub the skins off the nuts. (If you are using nuts that are already toasted, warm them in the oven a bit before going on to the next step.)

In a small bowl, mix together the brown sugar, rosemary, salt, orange zest, and hot sauce or vinegar. Add the warm toasted nuts and toss until well combined. Grease a 9 x 13-inch glass baking dish with vegetable oil and add the nut mixture. Bake, stirring every 5 minutes, for 15 minutes, until the sugar melts and the nuts are glazed. Don't keep the baking dish out of the oven too long when you stir, as the sugar may clump if it cools too much.

When the sugar has melted and coated all the nuts, remove the pan from the oven and cool completely. Break the hazelnuts apart and store in an airtight container at room temperature or in the refrigerator if the nuts get sticky.

## ELKDREAM BARS

There was a period of time when both of my children were in school, and I was spending an alarming portion of my grocery budget on granola bars, energy bars, and similar items that while an excellent alternative to cookies were nonetheless outrageously overpriced.
I came to call it the Tyranny of the Bar Aisle. Determined to overcome this tyranny (and to keep my budget in balance), I developed these Elkdream Bars and Fruit and Nut Energy Bars (page 224).

**2½ cups rolled oats (not quick-cook oats)**

**½ cup pumpkin seeds**

**¼ cup flax seeds**

**¼ cup sesame seeds**

**½ cup sunflower seeds**

**½ cup chopped hazelnuts**

Preheat the oven to 325°F.

In a large mixing bowl, mix together all of the above ingredients, then spread on a rimmed baking sheet and toast in the oven for 15 minutes. Pour back into the bowl. Leave the oven on, as you'll use it again in a few minutes.

Meanwhile, in a small saucepan combine:

**½ teaspoon ground ginger, or substitute cinnamon, cardamom, or other spices (optional)**

**1 teaspoon vanilla extract**

**½ cup honey**

**¼ cup peanut butter—either crunchy or smooth, or other nut butters such as sunflower seed butter, almond butter, or hazelnut butter**

**¼ cup brown sugar**

**2 to 3 Tablespoons butter**

Heat over medium-low heat, stirring until dissolved, then remove from the heat, so it doesn't burn. This is the glue that holds the bars together.

Pour the glue over the oat-nut mix, and add:

**1 cup dried cranberries, or your choice of chopped dried fruit**

Mix together very well.

Line a 9 x 13-inch glass dish with parchment paper (sometimes I brush the dish with oil first to help the parchment paper stick to it). Cut the paper long enough so it comes up all four sides of the pan (you can pleat the corners). Plop the oat mixture into the pan and press down *hard*. I put a piece of waxed paper on top and push down with a spatula, pressing it with my hand, all over the surface.

Bake for 15 minutes. Let it cool *completely*—this part is really important. Lift the whole arrangement out of the pan onto a cutting board (if you've left enough parchment paper, you can use it for a handle), and cut into whatever size bar you prefer. Wrap in waxed paper for easy snacking. Or, if you keep the bars together in one container, separate the layers with waxed paper.

## FRUIT AND NUT ENERGY BARS

These bars are not baked and contain no grains.

**1 cup almonds**

**1 cup dried apples, soaked in warm water if they are not very pliable**

**½ cup roughly chopped dates**

**1 cup roughly chopped figs—remove the hard stem end**

**¾ cup roughly chopped prunes**

**½ cup sunflower seeds**

**1 ounce very dark chocolate—85% if you can find it—chopped**

**3 Tablespoons ground flax seed**

**1 Tablespoon lemon juice**

In the bowl of a food processor, process the almonds until finely ground—but not to a paste. Add the fruit, a bit at a time, followed by the sunflower seeds, chocolate, and flax seeds. Add the lemon juice and process until the mixture comes together into a stiff dough.

Remove the dough to a cutting board or baking sheet covered with waxed paper. Knead it a few times until smooth. You may want to dampen or oil your hands as the dough will be sticky. Shape the dough into a ball, then flatten it to a disk. Cover with a sheet of waxed paper and roll out to ½-inch thick. Cut into bars in whatever shape suits you. Wrap each bar in a piece of waxed paper (you can reuse the paper you used to roll out the dough). Store in the refrigerator in an airtight container or plastic zip bag.

**VARIATIONS:** For a richer flavor, try toasting the nuts before you grind them. Vary the nuts in part or in total. Substitute other dried fruits—dried cranberries or dried cherries add a nice zing.

# SPREADS, SAUCES & SEASONINGS

With their heart-healthy oils, nuts and seeds do a great job of rounding out the flavor of many sauces, spreads, and seasonings found around the word. Think pesto from Italy and hummus from the Middle East... then add dukkah from Egypt, Romesco sauce from Spain, and furikake from Japan. We are all nuts!

## WALNUT-OLIVE SPREAD

A take-off on the Italian condiment *olivada*, this piquant spread can be whipped up in about 15 minutes. It stores well in a glass container in the refrigerator (add a film of olive oil over the top if storing more than a few days). A dab on a crostini or cracker will definitely wake up your taste buds before a meal. Try spreading some on a sandwich. Or thin the spread with olive oil and toss with hot pasta or steamed vegetables.

**2 cloves garlic**

**1 packed cup flat-leaf parsley**

**⅓ cup olive oil or as needed**

**½ teaspoon dried thyme**

**1 cup large green olives—try Castelvetrano if you can find them**

**1 cup toasted walnuts**

**2 Tablespoons lemon juice or to taste**

Place the garlic, parsley, and olive oil in a food processor and buzz a few times, scraping the bowl down once or twice, until the garlic is well integrated. Add the thyme, olives, and the nuts and process further, until all the ingredients are incorporated. You want the spread to have some texture, so don't process too much. Add the lemon juice to taste and more olive oil if desired.

**VARIATIONS:** Use black Gaeta olives or a mix of olives instead of green olives. A tablespoon or so of capers is a tasty addition. In the summer, add a small handful of fresh basil leaves. Or substitute red wine vinegar for the lemon juice.

## HAZELNUT HUMMUS

Contributed by Kronke Ranch, a small family farm located in Crow, Oregon. Replacing the traditional tahini with ground hazelnuts makes this hummus a very local treat!

Makes about 2½ cups.

**2 cups cooked garbanzo beans (see page 29)**

**2 to 3 Tablespoons garbanzo bean cooking water**

**1 cup ground toasted hazelnuts***

**¼ cup fresh lime juice**

**½ teaspoon cayenne pepper or to taste**

**2 to 3 Tablespoons olive oil**

**1 Tablespoon finely chopped garlic**

**1 teaspoon salt**

Place all ingredients in a food processor and process until smooth. Add more garlic, lime juice, or cayenne pepper to taste. If too thick, thin with more of the garbanzo bean cooking water or olive oil. Serve with still more olive oil drizzled on top, some chopped parsley, and a dusting of paprika if you are so inclined.

**VARIATION:** Soak a small handful of dried tomatoes in hot water for 10 minutes. Drain, then add to the food processor along with the garbanzo beans.

***TO PREPARE THE HAZELNUTS:** Spread the nuts on a baking sheet and toast them in a 325°F oven, for 10 to 15 minutes, until they are fragrant and golden. After they've cooled a bit, you can rub the nuts in a kitchen towel to remove the skins. Next, put the cooled toasted hazelnuts in the food processor and buzz until finely ground, but watch carefully that they don't turn into hazelnut butter (although some might argue that hazelnut butter is never a problem!).

## ELIN'S BASIL PESTO

Makes about 2½ cups.

**4 large cloves garlic, peeled**

**1 teaspoon salt**

**1 cup walnuts**

**2 cups freshly grated Parmesan cheese, or half Parmesan and half Pecorino Romano**

**1 cup flat-leaf parsley**

**4 cups packed fresh basil leaves**

**1 cup good-quality extra virgin olive oil**

Put the garlic, salt, walnuts, and cheese in a food processor and buzz briefly. Add the parsley, basil, and oil, and process until smooth. Freeze in ¼- or ½-cup containers or in ice-cube trays. Thaw and toss with pasta, slather on pizza, swirl into to soup, or spread on crostini.

**VARIATIONS:** Try other herbs or herb combinations. Omit the basil and use just parsley, for instance, or try half parsley and half cilantro. Greens can be used in lieu of, or in addition to the herbs. Arugula makes a lovely pesto. Kale leaves, minus their tough stems, can be made into pesto as well. Hazelnuts can be used instead of walnuts, as can sunflower seeds. In smaller quantities, pesto can be made with a mortar and pestle.

## ROMESCO SAUCE

Romesco sauce is somewhat like Spanish pesto. It is rich, aromatic, intoxicating, and a little goes a long way. As with so many traditional recipes, there are numerous ways to prepare it. The recipe is really a set of guidelines. Try it, and tinker with it until it suits you and your family, and then modify further according to the season. It is excellent on a piece of fish or a bit of grilled chicken or pork. Tuck some inside an omelet, or add it to a sandwich. Use it as a dip for fresh vegetables. Or simply stand at the counter with a bowl of the stuff and a spoon! With a thin layer of olive oil over the top, Romesco Sauce can be stored in the refrigerator for a few weeks. Or it can be frozen — try freezing it in an ice cube tray, and then adding a cube of frozen sauce to a pot of roasted squash soup!

Makes about 2 cups.

**1 to 1½ pounds Roma tomatoes**

**3 to 6 large cloves garlic, roughly chopped**

**1 to 2 large red peppers**

**⅛ to ¼ teaspoon red pepper flakes**

**½ cup hazelnuts, toasted and chopped roughly**

**1 teaspoon smoked Ancho chile powder**

**½ teaspoon chipotle chile powder**

**½ teaspoon smoked paprika**

**1 teaspoon salt, plus extra for roasting the tomatoes**

**1 slice day-old bread, toasted or fried in olive oil (optional)**

**2 Tablespoons or more sherry vinegar or red wine vinegar**

**⅓ cup extra virgin olive oil, plus extra for roasting the tomatoes**

Preheat the oven to 375°F.

Cut the tomatoes in half, and place them in a bowl. Sprinkle the garlic over the tomatoes. Drizzle with olive oil, sprinkle with a bit of salt, and toss. Spread the tomatoes, cut side up, on a rimmed baking sheet and roast for 15 minutes. Add the red peppers to the pan and roast another 15 minutes, until the tomatoes are shriveled and starting to blacken.

Scrape the tomatoes, red peppers, garlic, and accumulated juices from the pan to a food processor. Add the red pepper flakes, hazelnuts, spices, salt, and bread (if using). Process until blended, then in a steady stream, add the vinegar and the olive oil.

Taste and adjust seasonings, adding more red pepper flakes if you want a bit more kick, more smoked paprika or Ancho or chipotle chile powder if you like it smokier, more garlic if there is not enough to suit you, or a bit more vinegar if you prefer it tangier. If the sauce is too thick, thin it with more olive oil.

**VARIATIONS:** Most Romesco sauce recipes call for a slice or two of day-old crusty bread, such as ciabatta or other white bread. I have used a piece of sourdough rye and found it to be just as good. And the sauce is fine without any bread at all.

Substitute a cup of Slow-Roasted Tomatoes (page 54) when fresh tomatoes are out of season. You can also use frozen roasted red peppers. Lacking both fresh and frozen roasted tomatoes and peppers, a jar of roasted red peppers and a 15-ounce can of fire-roasted tomatoes make a fine substitute.

## DUKKAH

Dukkah is an Egyptian condiment made of crushed spices and ground nuts or seeds. Typically served with bread, which is dipped in olive oil and then in the bowl of dukkah, it is also an excellent adornment to a bowl of beans or grains, or on top of eggs, or dusted over a bowl of soup. Like so many traditional condiments, there are infinite variations on the composition. I've become fond of this version.

**½ Tablespoon cumin seeds, toasted**

**1 teaspoon fennel seeds**

**1 teaspoon sumac***

**Pinch red pepper flakes**

**½ teaspoon coarse salt**

**½ cup toasted hazelnuts, finely ground**

**½ cup toasted sesame seeds, ground**

**Pinch dry thyme**

**½ teaspoon smoked paprika**

Using a mortar and pestle or a spice grinder, grind together the cumin, fennel, sumac, red pepper flakes, and salt. Remove to a small bowl and mix in the ground hazelnuts, sesame seeds, thyme, and smoked paprika.

Store your dukkah in a covered container in the refrigerator so the nuts don't go rancid.

**VARIATIONS:** Try pumpkin seeds instead of hazelnuts. Substitute dry mint for the thyme. Add a teaspoon of toasted coriander seeds.

*Sumac is a ground dried berry that is found in a lot of Middle Eastern recipes. It has a very nice, fruity, tart flavor which is not quite as overpowering as that of a lemon. In addition to their very pleasant flavor, flakes from the sumac berry are a lovely deep-red color and make an excellent garnish.

## SORT-OF FURIKAKE

Furikake is a Japanese seaweed-based seasoning that is typically sprinkled on rice. It is also good on other types of cooked grain. I have been known to eat it out of hand as well—it is that addictive! This version includes non-traditional toasted flax seeds.

**2 sheets toasted nori seaweed**

**¼ cup sesame seeds—white or black**

**⅛ cup flax seeds**

**½ teaspoon coarse sea salt**

Toast the nori over a low flame, waving each sheet over the burner until it is crispy and darkens just a bit. Alternatively, toast it in a 300°F oven for 15 to 20 minutes. Then, cut or tear the nori into little bits.

Toast the sesame seeds and flax seeds in a dry skillet or a toaster oven set at low. If you are using white sesame seeds, they will turn golden when they are done. Black sesame seeds will simply smell toasty.

Using a mortar and pestle or a spice grinder, grind together half of the sesame seeds and all of the salt. Remove to a bowl and mix in the remaining sesame seeds, flax seeds, and nori bits.

Store in an airtight container.

**VARIATION**: Add a pinch or two of Japanese Sansho pepper to kick it up a bit.

# A FEW FINAL THOUGHTS

Coming to the end of writing this book, I sometimes feel that I know less about cooking with beans, grains, nuts, and seeds than I did when I started. Or perhaps more accurately, I am now aware of the vast repertoire for using these wonderful foods. I've barely scratched the surface in this collection of recipes!

It seems that in the U.S. and many other "developed" countries, we have, in the pursuit of making cooking easier and faster, lost a great deal of the accumulated knowledge of how to feed ourselves that our ancestors—even just a few generations back—assumed to be common knowledge. Perhaps part of our work as we move forward is to look backward and reclaim those skills.

I need to stop somewhere, though. Please enjoy these recipes, and then continue reading and experimenting and finding ways to regain the wisdom of how to bring good food to the table to nourish those you love.

# CONTRIBUTORS

This book is a collection of the inspirations, ideas, accumulated knowledge, and pieces of advice of a great many people. Following are the names of those to whom specific recipes should be attributed. Many others who contributed to the book are not listed here by name but are no less appreciated.

**Carol and Anthony Boutard** own Ayers Creek Farm, a 144-acre organic market farm near Portland, where they specialize in reviving long-lost crops and bringing little-known varieties to market. They leave a trail of inspired and impassioned bean and grain aficionados wherever they go.

**Jennifer Burns Bright** is involved in many food adventures in and around Eugene. She is one of the voices on KLCC's *Food For Thought* and the author of the blog *Culinaria Eugenius*. Follow her on culinariaeugenius.wordpress.com.

**Linda Colwell** is a French-trained chef in Portland and a frequent visitor at Ayers Creek Farm, where she not only helps with the harvest, she also facilitates recovery from a stint in the field by cooking up the fruits of their collective labors in a most delectable fashion.

**Andrea Davis** of King Valley Gardens in Kings Valley, Oregon. Her recipe for corn pones came to me via Sarah Kreeger of Open Oak Farms (Sweet Home, Oregon).

**Katherine Deumling** is the owner and operator of Cook With What You Have, a small business in Portland committed to making cooking a regular, fun, and creative part of life. In addition to teaching cooking classes, she also works with local CSA farms, creating weekly customized recipe packets for members. Katherine is also involved with Slow Food USA. Find out more about her classes at www.cookwithwhatyouhave.com.

**Nabiha Doolittle** worked with me at the Oregon Bach Festival. We had great fun talking about the various ways her Pakistani family cooks beans and tracking down the English translations for their many herbs and spices.

**Lynne Fessenden** is executive director of the Willamette Farm and Food Coalition and is instrumental in so many areas of bringing together farmers, their food, and the people who eat it that I can't possibly list them all. Sometimes she even finds time to cook!

**Karen Guillemin** is the woman behind the Fairmount Neighbors website and a true bean and grain aficionado. I always look forward to reading her blog to see what was cooking in the Guillemin household over the weekend. Her recipes can be found at www.fairmountmarket.blogspot.com.

**Mary Ann Jasper** of Greenwillow Grains. Greenwillow Grains is an organic grain mill specializing in stone-ground flour, rolled grain, dried beans, and edible seeds grown by Harry Stalford and Willow Coberly of Stalford Seed Farms in the Willamette Valley.

Open Oak Farm is stewarded by farmers **Sarah Kleeger**, **Andrew Still**, and **Cooper Boydston**, who are all passionate about growing (and getting others to grow) heritage staple crops. The farm is also the home of Adaptive Seeds.

**Daniel Klein and Mirra Fine** produce *The Perennial Plate*, an online documentary series dedicated to socially responsible and adventurous eating. Daniel and Mirra began by exploring Minnesota, then the U.S., and are now traveling the world, exploring the wonders, complexities, and stories behind the ever more connected food system. Their videos, blog entries, and recipes can be found at www.theperennialplate.com.

**Elke Kronke** and her husband own Kronke Ranch, a small orchard situated in the hills outside Eugene that produces high-quality hazelnuts offered primarily at the Eugene Farmers Market. They do most of their cultivation and harvesting by hand.

**Krista Rome** started the Backyard Bean and Grain Project in 2008. Her focus is on seed trials and teaching others in western Washington (and beyond) how to grow dry beans and grains and oilseed crops in a low-tech manner, so that anyone can feel empowered to grow their own staple crops. Find out more about her work at www.backyardbeanandgrains.com.

**Mark and Joey Running** of Running Wild Rice sell wild rice grown and milled in Brownsville, Oregon. You can find their rice at eugenelocalfoods.com, and you can follow them on Facebook.

**Lisa Skopil** is a talented pastry chef in Eugene. Her father, Royce Saltzman, is the director emeritus of the Oregon Bach Festival. Over the years, many of us in the OBF family have been treated to Lisa's tempting delicacies.

**Heidi Tunnell**, of Heidi Tunnell Catering in Creswell, is a quiet force of nature, who started a catering company in this small town south of Eugene, where she serves up Tuesday lunches and Thursday night dinners, family-style in a refurbished church, and holds festive barn dinners in her parents' nearby barn.

**Dawn Woodward** of Evelyn's Crackers in Ontario, Canada. Her recipe for spelt-hazelnut cookies came to me via Sue Hunton of Camas Country Mill in Eugene, Oregon.

# REFERENCES AND RESOURCES

Still hungry? The following books and websites have been fantastic sources of inspiration and knowledge for me. Check them out!

**GOOD BOOKS**

Boutard, Anthony. *Beautiful Corn*. British Columbia: New Society Publishers, 2012.

Boyce, Kim. *Good to the Grain*. New York: Stewart, Tabori & Chang, 2010.

Della Croce, Julia. *The Classic Italian Cookbook*. New York: DK Publishing, Inc., 1996.

Deppe, Carol. *The Resilient Gardener*. White River Junction: Chelsea Green, 2010.

Fallon, Sally. *Nourishing Traditions*. Washington: New Trends Publishing, 1999.

Ferrigno, Ursula. *Truly Italian*. London: Mitchell Beazley, 2002.

Greene, Bert. *The Grains Cookbook*. New York: Workman Publishing, 1988.

Katz, Sandor Elliz. *Wild Fermentation*. White River Junction: Chelsea Green, 2003.

Landon, Sheryl and Mel. *The Versatile Grain and the Elegant Bean*. New York: Simon & Schuster, 1992.

Lawson, Tracy. *A Year in the Village of Eternity*. New York: Bloomsbury, 2011.

Roberts-Dominguez, Jan. *Oregon Hazelnut Country*. Aurora: Hazelnut Marketing Board, 2010.

Robertson, Lauren. *The Laurel's Kitchen Bread Book*. New York: Random House, Inc., 1984.

Sando, Steve and Vanessa Barrington. *Heirloom Beans*. San Francisco: Chronicle Books, 2008.

Sokolov, Raymond. *With the Grain*. New York: Alfred A. Knopf, 1996.

Speck, Maria. *Ancient Grains for Modern Meals*. Berkeley: Ten Speed Press, 2011.

Waters, Alice. *The Art of Simple Food*. New York: Clarkson Potter Publishers, 2007.

Weinstein, Bruce and Mark Scarbrough. *Grain Mains*. New York: Rodale, Inc., 2012.

## GREAT RESOURCES

By no means an exhaustive list, the following are a few of the many purveyors of beans and grains that abound in the Pacific Northwest, plus a few other helpful sites.

**Bluebird Grains Farm.** A great source of organically grown grains and flours, located in Winthrop, Washington. www.bluebirdgrainfarms.com

**Bob's Red Mill.** One of the few mills still using traditional quartz grinding stones, Bob and his capable staff have been providing a wide variety of grains and flours since 1978. www.bobsredmill.com

**Camas Country Mill.** Tom and Sue Hunton are third-generation family farmers who have been instrumental in re-establishing locally grown and milled beans and grains in the Pacific Northwest. Their wares can be found at many farmers markets, at Eugene Local Foods, and online. www.camascountrymill.com

**Cultures for Health.** Need a sourdough starter or more information about fermentation? This is a great site! www.culturesforhealth.com

**Eugene Local Foods.** An online year-round farmers market serving the Willamette Valley. www.eugenelocalfoods.com

**Greenwillow Grains** mills and sells grains, beans, and edible seeds grown in the Willamette Valley by Harry Stalford and his wife, Willow Coberly. Harry and Willow are part of the original group of farmers involved in the Willamette Valley Bean and Grain Coalition. www.greenwillowgrains.com

**Hillsdale Farmers Market.** If you are in Portland and want to avail yourself of the wonderful beans and grains grown by Ayers Creek Farm, and perhaps catch a cooking demonstration by Katherine Deumling, head on over to the Hillsdale Farmers Market. www.hillsdalefarmersmarket.com

**Lonesome Whistle Farm.** Jeff Broadie and Kasey White's heirloom beans and grains can be found at many farmers markets in the South Willamette Valley. They sell CSA shares as well. www.lonesomewhistlefarm.com

**Open Oak Farm** and **Adaptive Seeds.** CSA shares of beans, grains, and winter vegetables are available through Open Oak Farm. Seeds for the home gardener can be found through Adaptive Seeds. www.openoakfarm.com and www.adaptiveseeds.com

**Rancho Gordo** is located in California, not the Pacific Northwest, but their website is so inspiring (and their beans so tempting) that it seems appropriate to include them. www.ranchogordo.com

**Whole Grains Council.** A wonderful source for information about grains in general. www.wholegrainscouncil.org

**Willamette Valley Bean & Grain Coalition.** Dan Armstrong has been chronicling the growth of the Coalition since its inception. His website is a wealth of information. www.mudcitypress.com/beanandgrain.html

**Zürsun Idaho Heirloom Beans.** Although Idaho is not technically part of the Pacific Northwest, I've included their website as it is a great place to read about a huge variety of beans. Their beans can sometimes be found in local grocery stores. www.zursunbeans.com

# INDEX

**ALMONDS**
Bean Salad with Wheat Berries and Quinoa, 90
Fruit and Nut Energy Bars, 224
Panforte, 218
Red Pepper Sauce for Ireland Creek Annie Bruschetta, 41
Wheat Berry Pilaf, 151
Winter Squash Stew with Purple Barley, 172

**AMARANTH**
*About*, 112
Crockpot Grain Party Porridge, 121

**ANAHEIM CHILE**, see Chile, Anaheim

**ANCHOVIES**
Mediterranean Lentil Tapenade, 37

**APPETIZERS**
Arikara Bean Pâté with Toasted Spices, 34
Ceci Fritta, 36
Dried Fruit and Nut Crostini, 212
Farinata, 38
Hazelnut Crackers, 214
Hazelnut Hummus, 226
Ireland Creek Annie Bean Bruschetta, 40
Italian Suppli, 150
Mediterranean Lentil Tapenade, 37
Overnight Oatcakes, 180
Romesco Sauce, 228
Spicy Rosemary Hazelnuts with Orange Zest, 221
Walnut-Olive Spread, 225
Winter White Bean Dip with Turnips, Lemon & Sage, 42

**APPLES, DRIED**
Fruit and Nut Energy Bars, 224
Fruit Compote, 191
Panforte, 218
Sugar Plums, 220

**APPLES, FRESH**
Dolce di Grano, 184
Fruit Compote, 191
Purple Barley Salad with Apples and Celery, 154
Spicy Nutty Apple Rye Muffins, 178
Teff and Ricotta Pancakes with Apple Topping, 127
Toasted Bulgur Wheat Porridge with Apples, 122
Wheat Berry Salad with Broccoli, Apple, Hazelnuts & Smoked Salmon, 158

**APRICOTS, DRIED**
Dolce di Grano, 184
Panforte, 218
Sugar Plums, 220

**ARIKARA BEANS**
Arikara Bean Pâté with Toasted Spices, 34
Arikara Beans with Tomatillo Pork, 57
Mediterranean-Style Pasta and Beans, 68
Winter White Bean Dip with Turnips, Lemon & Sage, 42

**ARUGULA**
Arugula Pesto, 169
Roast Roots 'n Rye, 156

**BARLEY**
Barley Beef Stew with Mushrooms, 162
Barley Mushroom Terrine, 136
Bean Burgers with Greens 'n Grains, 84
Crockpot Grain Party Porridge, 121
Golden Barley Risotto with Wild Mushrooms, 148
Golden Hulless Barley Pudding with Fruit Compote, 190
Italian Suppli, 150
Purple Barley Salad with Apples and Celery, 154
Salmon and Barley Cakes, 144

Summer Grain Salad, 160
Winter Squash Stew with Purple
   Barley, 172

**BARS**
Elkdream Bars, 222
Fruit and Nut Energy Bars, 224

**BASIL**
Beans with Basil Pesto, 46
Beans with Tomato Pistou, 47
Elin's Basil Pesto, 227
Lemon-Walnut Cilantro Sauce, 44
Savory Teffolenta, 134

**BEANS,** see also specific varieties
*Bean Cooking Basics*, 29
*Families*, 24
*Heirloom*, 26
*Sprouting*, 28

**BEEF**
Barley Beef Stew with Mushrooms, 162
Joanna's Chili, 66
Polenta Pasticciata di Mama Elin, 132
Tongue, in Hominy with Chile and
   Tomato Braised Meat, 196

**BISCUITS**
Chef Zachary's Unbelievable
   Buttermilk Biscuits, 182

**BLACK BEANS**
Bean Burgers with Greens 'n Grains, 84
Black Bean, Chorizo & Rice Stew, 70
Black Bean Patties, 86
Chocolate Baked Rio Zape Beans, 76
Daniel's Black Beans, 45

**BORLOTTI BEANS,** see also
Cranberry Beans
Basic Bean Salad, 89
Bean Salad with Wheat Berries
   and Quinoa, 90
Beans with Pesto and Pistou, 46
Braised Rosso di Lucca Beans with
   Rosemary and Thyme, 48
Cranberry Beans Simmered with
   Sage, Sausages & Tomatoes, 64

Ribollita, 102
Spring Bean Salad, 93

**BORLOTTO DEL VALDARNO,**
see also Borlotti Beans
Beans with Pesto and Pistou, 46

**BREAD**
Dried Fruit and Nut Crostini, 212
Farmor's Limpa, 202
Ribollita, 102
Sourdough Rye Bread, 206
Sourdough Rye Starter, 204

**BREADCRUMBS,** see also Panko
Black Bean Patties, 86

**BREAKFAST,** see also Porridge,
Pancakes
*Grains for*, 118
Spicy Nutty Apple Rye Muffins, 178

**BRIGHTSTONE BEANS,** see also
Kidney Beans
Joanna's Chili, 66
Winter Squash Stew with Purple
   Barley, 172

**BROCCOLI**
Bean Salad with Wheat Berries
   and Quinoa, 90
Mediterranean-Style Pasta and
   Beans, 68
Roast Roots 'n Rye, 156
Wheat Berry Salad with Broccoli,
   Apple, Hazelnuts & Smoked
   Salmon, 158

**BRUSCHETTA**
Ireland Creek Annie Bean
   Bruschetta, 40

**BRUSSELS SPROUTS**
Roast Roots 'n Rye, 156

**BUCKWHEAT**
*About*, 114
Buckwheat Crêpes, 138
Chia Seed and Buckwheat
   Pancakes, 125

**BULGUR WHEAT**
*About*, 116
Bulgur Wheat Soup with Lentils and Winter Greens, 164
Frikeh and Buttermilk Soup, 166
Toasted Bulgur Wheat Porridge with Apples, 122

**BUTTERMILK**
Frikeh and Buttermilk Soup, 166

**CABBAGE**
Crunchy Cabbage, Carrot & Radish Slaw, 59
Minestrone with Wheat Berries and Arugula Pesto, 168
Ribollita, 102

**CALYPSO BEANS**
Calypso Beans with Coconut Milk, Ginger & Black Mustard Seeds, 50

**CANNELLINI BEANS**
Basic Bean Salad, 89
Bean Salad with Wheat Berries and Quinoa, 90
Cannellini Beans with Grilled Tuna, 60
Mediterranean-Style Pasta and Beans, 68
Ribollita, 102
Spring Bean Salad, 93
Winter White Bean Dip with Turnips, Lemon & Sage, 42

**CARROT**
Barley Beef Stew with Mushrooms, 162
Crunchy Cabbage, Carrot & Radish Slaw, 59
*In soffritto*, 30
North African-Style Garbanzo Bean Stew, 100
Roast Roots 'n Rye, 156

**CAULIFLOWER**
Winter Squash Stew with Purple Barley, 172

**CELERIAC (CELERY ROOT)**
Indian Woman Yellow Bean Soup with Hardy Greens, 98
Minestrone with Wheat Berries and Arugula Pesto, 168
Roast Roots 'n Rye, 156
Winter White Bean Dip with Turnips, Lemon & Sage, 42

**CELERY**
*In soffritto*, 30
Barley Beef Stew with Mushrooms, 162
Purple Barley Salad with Apples and Celery, 154
Wheat Berry Salad with Broccoli, Apple, Hazelnuts & Smoked Salmon, 158

**CEREAL, HOT**, see Porridge

**CHARD (SWISS CHARD)**
Barley Beef Stew with Mushrooms, 162
Bean Burgers with Greens 'n Grains, 84
Roast Roots 'n Rye, 156
Roasted Garbanzos with Garlic and Greens, 62

**CHEROKEE TRAIL OF TEARS BEANS,** see also Black Beans
Daniel's Black Beans, 45

**CHERRIES, DRIED**
Dolce di Grano, 184
Panforte, 218
Sugar Plums, 220

**CHIA SEEDS**
Chia Seed and Buckwheat Pancakes, 125

**CHICKEN**
Indian Woman Yellow Bean Soup with Hardy Greens, 98
Posole Soup with Beans, 201

**CHICKPEAS,** see Garbanzo Beans

**CHILE, ANAHEIM**
Black Bean Patties, 86
Chocolate Baked Rio Zape Beans, 76

Cilantro and Toasted Pumpkin
   Seed Sauce, 72
Posole Soup with Beans, 201

**CHILE, CHIPOTLE**
Chocolate Baked Rio Zape Beans, 76

**CHILES, DRIED**
Hominy with Chile and Tomato
   Braised Meat, 196

**CHILES, JALAPEÑO**
Arikara Beans with Tomatillo Pork, 57
Basic Salsa, 199
Cilantro and Toasted Pumpkin Seed
   Sauce, 72
Quick Tomatillo Salsa, 87

**CHILE, PASILLA**
Jennifer's Sort-of Posole, 200
Posole Soup with Beans, 201

**CHILE, POBLANO**
Cilantro and Toasted Pumpkin
   Seed Sauce, 72
Posole Soup with Beans, 201

**CHORIZO**
Black Bean, Chorizo & Rice Stew, 70

**CILANTRO**
Arikara Beans with Tomatillo Pork, 57
Basic Salsa, 199
Cilantro and Toasted Pumpkin
   Seed Sauce, 70
Lemon-Walnut Cilantro Sauce, 44
Nabiha's Father's Way with Lentils, 52
Quick Tomatillo Salsa, 87

**COLLARD GREENS,** see also Greens
Indian Woman Yellow Bean Soup with
   Hardy Greens, 98

**COOKIES,** see also Bars
Claudia's Hazelnut Cookies, 217
Farmor's Hazelnut Cookies, 216
Not Your Nonna's Biscotti, 188
Spelt-Hazelnut Cookies, 185
Teff Chocolate Chip Cookies,
   Two Ways, 186

**CORN**
*About*, 115
Hominy, 195
Nixtamal, 194
Tortillas, 198

**CORNMEAL**
Basic Polenta, 131
Basic Whole Grain Pancakes, 124
Corn Crisps, 175
Corn Pones, 176
Cornmeal Pancakes, 129
Indian Pudding, 192
Polenta Pasticciata di Mama Elin, 132
Spoonbread, 177

**CRAB**
Crab and Kale Crêpe Filling, 140

**CRACKERS**
Dried Fruit and Nut Crostini, 212
Hazelnut Crackers, 214
Overnight Oatcakes, 180

**CRANBERRY BEANS,** see also Borlotti,
Borlotto del Valdarno, Rosso di Lucca Beans
Basic Bean Salad, 89
Beans with Pesto and Pistou, 46
Braised Rosso di Lucca Beans with
   Rosemary and Thyme, 48
Cranberry Beans & Rye Patties with
   Sage & Walnuts, 80
Cranberry Beans Simmered with Sage,
   Sausages & Tomatoes, 64
Minestrone with Wheat Berries and
   Arugula Pesto, 168
Spring Bean Salad, 93

**CRANBERRIES, DRIED**
Dolce di Grano, 184
Dried Fruit and Nut Crostini, 212
Elkdream Bars, 222
Panforte, 218
Purple Barley Salad with Apples
   and Celery, 154
Roast Roots 'n Rye, 156
Wild Rice with Cranberries and
   Caramelized Onions, 152

**CREPES**
Buckwheat Crêpes, 138
Crab and Kale Crêpe Filling, 140
*Filling, ideas for,* 139
Pear, Prune & Armagnac Crêpe Filling, 141

**CUCUMBER**
Cannellini Beans with Grilled Tuna, 60
Raita for Curried Lentil Soup, 94
Summer Grain Salad, 160
Tzatziki, 83

**CURRANTS,** see also Raisins
North African-Style Garbanzo Bean Stew, 100
Roast Roots 'n Rye, 156

**DATES**
Fruit and Nut Energy Bars, 224
Sugar Plums, 220

**DESSERT**
A Simple Fruit Crumble, 183
Claudia's Hazelnut Cookies, 217
Dolce di Grano, 184
Farmor's Hazelnut Cookies, 216
Golden Hulless Barley Pudding with Fruit Compote, 190
Indian Pudding, 192
Not Your Nonna's Biscotti, 188
Panforte, 218
Spelt-Hazelnut Cookies, 185
Sugar Plums, 220
Teff Chocolate Chip Cookies, Two Ways, 186

**DIPS AND PATES,** see also Sauces, Spreads & Pesto
Arikara Bean Pâté with Toasted Spices, 34
Hazelnut Hummus, 226
Ireland Creek Annie Bean Bruschetta, 40
Mediterranean Lentil Tapenade, 37
Winter White Bean Dip with Turnips, Lemon & Sage, 42

**DUTCH BULLET BEANS**
Winter White Bean Dip with Turnips, Lemon & Sage, 42

**EGGPLANT**
Late Summer Lentil Stew with Roasted Vegetables, 96
Savory Teffolenta, 134

**EGGS**
*How to poach,* 143
Spring Bean Salad, 93
Wheat Berries Arrabiata with Poached Eggs, 142
Wheat Berry Salad with Broccoli, Apple, Hazelnuts & Smoked Salmon, 158

**EMMER,** see Farro

**EYE OF THE TIGER BEANS,** see also Pinto Beans
Arikara Beans with Tomatillo Pork, 57
Farinata, 38
Posole Soup with Beans, 201

**FARRO**
Dolce di Grano, 184
Golden Barley Risotto with Wild Mushrooms, 148
Summer Grain Salad, 160

**FENNEL BULB**
Minestrone with Wheat Berries and Arugula Pesto, 168
Purple Barley Salad with Apples and Celery, 154
Spring Bean Salad, 93

**FIGS, DRIED**
Dried Fruit and Nut Crostini, 212
Fruit and Nut Energy Bars, 224
Panforte, 218
Sugar Plums, 220

**FILBERTS,** see Hazelnuts

**FISH,** see Anchovies, Crab, Salmon, Tuna

**FLAGEOLET BEANS**
Bean Salad with Wheat Berries and Quinoa, 90

**FLAX SEED**
Dried Fruit and Nut Crostini, 212
Elkdream Bars, 222
Fruit and Nut Energy Bars, 224
Teff, Flax & Oatmeal Porridge, 123
Sort-of Furikake, 231

**FRIKEH**
Frikeh and Buttermilk Soup, 166
Frikeh Pilaf, 166
Summer Grain Salad, 160

**GARBANZO BEANS**
Bean Burgers with Greens 'n Grains, 84
Bean Salad with Wheat Berries and Quinoa, 90
Ceci Fritta, 36
Farinata, 38
Garbanzo Bean Salad with Summer Herbs, 92
Hazelnut Hummus, 226
Homemade Falafel, 82
Lemony Garbanzo Bean Soup, 104
North African-Style Garbanzo Bean Stew, 100
Roasted Garbanzos with Garlic and Greens, 62

**GINGER**
*About using fresh*, 101
Bean Burgers with Greens 'n Grains, 84
Calypso Beans with Coconut Milk, Ginger & Black Mustard Seeds, 50
Curried Lentil Soup, 95
Nabiha's Father's Way with Lentils, 52
North African-Style Garbanzo Bean Stew, 100
Tarka, Nabiha's Father's, 53
Tarka, Simple, 51

**GRAINS**, See also Amaranth, Buckwheat, Bulgur Wheat, Corn, Millet, Quinoa, Teff
Basic Big Berry Grain Cooking, 111
*Grain types*, 109
*Sprouting*, 117

**GREENS**, see also Arugula, Cabbage, Chard, Collards, Kale, Mustard Greens
Bean Burgers with Greens 'n Grains, 84
Bulgur Wheat Soup with Lentils and Winter Greens, 164
Indian Woman Yellow Bean Soup with Hardy Greens, 98
Roasted Garbanzos with Garlic and Greens, 62
Roast Roots 'n Rye, 156

**HAZELNUTS**
Claudia's Hazelnut Cookies, 217
Elkdream Bars, 222
Farmor's Hazelnut Cookies, 216
Dried Fruit and Nut Crostini, 212
Dukkah, 230
*Harvesting*, 209
Hazelnut Crackers, 214
Hazelnut Hummus, 226
Spicy Nutty Apple Rye Muffins, 178
Panforte, 218
*Roasting in the shell*, 159
Romesco Sauce, 228
Spelt-Hazelnut Cookies, 185
Spicy Rosemary Hazelnuts with Orange Zest, 221
Spring Bean Salad, 93
Sugar Plums, 220
Wheat Berry Pilaf, 151
Wheat Berry Salad with Broccoli, Apple, Hazelnuts & Smoked Salmon, 158
Wild Rice with Cranberries and Caramelized Onions, 152

**HOMINY**, see Corn

**HUTTERITE SOUP BEANS**
Indian Woman Yellow Bean Soup with Hardy Greens, 98
Winter White Bean Dip with Turnips, Lemon & Sage, 42

**INDIAN WOMAN YELLOW BEANS**
Basic Bean Salad, 89
Indian Woman Yellow Bean Soup with Hardy Greens, 98

Mediterranean-Style Pasta and
  Beans, 68
Winter Squash Stew with Purple
  Barley, 172

**IRELAND CREEK ANNIE BEANS**
Ireland Creek Annie Bean Bruschetta, 40

**JALAPEÑO,** see Chile, Jalapeño

**KALE**
Barley Beef Stew with Mushrooms, 162
Bean Burgers with Greens 'n Grains, 84
Bean Salad with Wheat Berries and
  Quinoa, 90
Bulgur Wheat Soup with Lentils
  and Winter Greens, 164
Crab and Kale Crêpe Filling, 140
Cranberry Beans Simmered with Sage,
  Sausages & Tomatoes, 64
Indian Woman Yellow Bean Soup
  with Hardy Greens, 98
Kale Chips, 161
Mediterranean-Style Pasta and Beans, 68
Ribollita, 102
Roast Roots 'n Rye, 156
Roasted Garbanzos with Garlic
  and Greens, 62

**KAMUT**
Summer Grain Salad, 160

**KIDNEY BEANS,** see also Brightstone Beans
Joanna's Chili, 66

**LAMB**
Barley Beef Stew with Mushrooms, 162

**LEEKS**
Crab and Kale Crêpe Filling, 140

**LENTILS**
Bulgur Wheat Soup with Lentils
  and Winter Greens, 164
Curried Lentil Soup, 95
Late Summer Lentil Stew with
  Roasted Vegetables, 96
Mediterranean Lentil Tapenade, 37
Nabiha's Father's Way with Lentils, 52

**MILLET**
*About*, 112
Bean Burgers with Greens 'n Grains, 84
Crockpot Grain Party Porridge, 121

**MUFFINS**
Spicy Nutty Apple Rye Muffins, 178

**MUSHROOMS**
Barley Beef Stew with Mushrooms, 162
Barley Mushroom Terrine, 136
Golden Barley Risotto with Wild
  Mushrooms, 148
Mushroom Cream Garnish, 146
Polenta Pasticciata di Mama Elin, 132

**MUSTARD GREENS**
Barley Beef Stew with Mushrooms, 162
Roast Roots 'n Rye, 156

**NAVY BEANS**
Eunice's Yellow-Eyed Baked Beans, 74

**NIXTAMAL,** see Corn

**NUT BUTTERS**
Elkdream Bars, 222
*In porridge*, 119
Teff Chocolate Chip Cookies,
  Version I, 186

**NUTS**
*Harvesting*, 209
*Sprouting*, 211
*Toasting*, 211

**OAT BERRIES (GROATS)**
Wheat Berries Arrabiata with
  Poached Eggs, 142
Wheat Berry Pilaf, 151

**OAT FLOUR**
Overnight Oatcakes, 180

**OATS (ROLLED, STEEL-CUT)**
Elkdream Bars, 222
A Simple Fruit Crumble, 183
Crockpot Grain Party Porridge, 121
Oatmeal, 119
Overnight Oatcakes, 180

Overnight Oatmeal-Sesame Pancakes, 128
Teff, Flax & Oatmeal Porridge, 123

**OLIVES**
Cannellini Beans with Grilled Tuna, 60
Mediterranean Lentil Tapenade, 37
Mediterranean-Style Pasta and Beans, 68
Summer Grain Salad, 160
Walnut-Olive Spread, 225

**ONIONS**
Basic Bean Salad, 89
In *soffritto*, 30
Pickled Onions, 58
Roast Roots 'n Rye, 156
Summer Grain Salad, 160
Wild Rice with Cranberries and Caramelized Onions, 152

**ORCA BEANS,** see Calypso Beans

**PANCAKES**
Basic Whole Grain Pancakes, 124
Cornmeal Pancakes, 129
Overnight Oatmeal-Sesame Pancakes, 128
Teff and Ricotta Pancakes with Apple Topping, 126

**PANKO**
Homemade Panko, 81

**PARSLEY**
Parsley Pesto, 79
Lemon-Walnut Cilantro Sauce, 44

**PARSNIP**
Barley Beef Stew with Mushrooms, 162
Minestrone with Wheat Berries and Arugula Pesto, 168
Roast Roots 'n Rye, 156

**PASTA**
Mediterranean-Style Pasta and Beans, 68

**PEARS**
Pear, Prune & Armagnac Crêpe Filling, 141
Spicy Nutty Apple Rye Muffins, 178

**PEPPERS, JALAPEÑO,** see Chiles, Jalapeño

**PEPPERS, SWEET**
Basic Bean Salad, 89
Bean Salad with Wheat Berries and Quinoa, 90
Crunchy Cabbage, Carrot & Radish Slaw, 59
Mediterranean-Style Pasta and Beans, 68
Red Pepper Sauce for Ireland Creek Annie Bruschetta, 41
Romesco Sauce, 228
Savory Teffolenta, 134
Spanish Sofrito Sauce, 55
Summer Grain Salad, 160
Wheat Berries Arrabiata with Poached Eggs, 142

**PESTO,** see Sauces, Spreads & Pesto

**PINTO BEANS,** see also Rio Zape Beans, Eye of the Tiger Beans
Arikara Beans with Tomatillo Pork, 57
Black Bean, Chorizo & Rice Stew, 70
Chocolate Baked Rio Zape Beans, 76
Posole Soup with Beans, 201

**PLUMS**
Dolce di Grano, 184
Fruit Compote, 191

**POLENTA**
Basic Polenta, 131
Polenta Crostini, 132

**PORRIDGE**
Crockpot Grain Party Porridge, 121
Oatmeal, 119
Teff, Flax & Oatmeal Porridge, 123
Toasted Bulgur Wheat Porridge with Apples, 122

**PORK**
Arikara Beans with Tomatillo Pork, 57
Ham Hock, in cooking beans, 30
Hominy with Chili and Tomato Braised Meat, 196
Jennifer's Sort-of Posole, 200
Polenta Pasticciata di Mama Elin, 132
Posole Soup with Beans, 201
Salt Pork, in Eunice's Yellow-Eyed Baked Beans, 74

**POTATOES**
Indian Woman Yellow Bean Soup with Hardy Greens, 98

**PRUNES**
Fruit and Nut Energy Bars, 224
Fruit Compote, 191
Pear, Prune & Armagnac Crêpe Filling, 141
Sugar Plums, 220

**PUDDING**
Golden Hulless Barley Pudding with Fruit Compote, 190
Indian Pudding, 192

**PUMPKIN SEEDS**
Cilantro and Toasted Pumpkin Seed Sauce, 72
Dried Fruit and Nut Crostini, 212
Elkdream Bars, 222

**QUINOA**
About, 113
Bean Salad with Wheat Berries and Quinoa, 90
Black Bean Patties, 86
Crockpot Grain Party Porridge, 121
Smoky Tomato Soup with Quinoa, 170

**RADISH**
Crunchy Cabbage, Carrot & Radish Slaw, 59
Spring Bean Salad, 93
Summer Grain Salad, 160

**RAISINS**
Fruit Compote, 191

North African-Style Garbanzo Bean Stew, 100

**RICE, BROWN**
Bean Burgers with Greens 'n Grains, 84
Black Bean, Chorizo & Rice Stew, 70
Crockpot Grain Party Porridge, 121
Curried Lentil Soup, 95
Wild Rice with Cranberries and Caramelized Onions, 152

**RICE, WILD**
About, 116
Wheat Berry Salad with Broccoli, Apple, Hazelnuts & Smoked Salmon, 158
Wild Rice with Cranberries and Caramelized Onions, 152

**RIO ZAPE BEANS**, see also Pinto Beans
Chocolate Baked Rio Zape Beans, 76
Posole Soup with Beans, 201

**ROSSO DI LUCCA BEANS**
Braised Rosso di Lucca Beans with Rosemary and Thyme, 48

**RUTABAGA**
Roast Roots 'n Rye, 156
Winter White Bean Dip with Turnips, Lemon & Sage, 42

**RYE, BERRIES**
Cranberry Beans & Rye Patties with Sage & Walnuts, 80
Roast Roots 'n Rye, 156
Summer Grain Salad, 160
Wheat Berries Arrabiata with Poached Eggs, 142
Wheat Berry Pilaf, 151

**RYE, FLOUR**
A Simple Fruit Crumble, 183
Basic Whole Grain Pancakes, 124
Dried Fruit and Nut Crostini, 212
Farmor's Limpa, 202
Hazelnut Crackers, 214
Not Your Nonna's Biscotti, 188
Sourdough Rye Bread, 206
Spicy Nutty Apple Rye Muffins, 178

**SALAD,** see also Slaw
Basic Bean Salad, 89
Bean Salad with Wheat Berries and Quinoa, 90
Cannellini Beans with Fresh Grilled Tuna, 60
Garbanzo Bean Salad with Summer Herbs, 92
*Grain Salads*, 153
Purple Barley Salad with Apples and Celery, 154
Roast Roots 'n Rye, 156
Spring Bean Salad, 93
Summer Grain Salad, 160
Wheat Berry Salad with Broccoli, Apple, Hazelnuts & Smoked Salmon, 158

**SALMON**
Roast Roots 'n Rye, 156
Salmon and Barley Cakes, 144
Wheat Berry Salad with Broccoli, Apple, Hazelnuts & Smoked Salmon, 158

**SALSA**
Basic Salsa, 199
Quick Tomatillo Salsa, 87

**SAUCES, SPREADS & PESTO**
Arugula Pesto, 169
Beans with Tomato Pistou, 47
Cilantro and Toasted Pumpkin Seed Sauce, 72
Elin's Basil Pesto, 227
Ireland Creek Annie Bean Spread, 40
Lemon-Dill Yoghurt Sauce, 146
Lemon-Garlic Tahini Sauce, 83
Lemon-Walnut Cilantro Sauce, 44
Mediterranean Lentil Tapenade, 37
Mushroom Cream Garnish, 146
Parsley Pesto, 79
Red Pepper Sauce for Ireland Creek Annie Bruschetta, 41
Romesco Sauce, 228
Spanish Sofrito Sauce, 55
Tzatziki, 83
Walnut-Olive Spread, 225

**SAUSAGE**
Black Bean, Chorizo & Rice Stew, 70
Indian Woman Yellow Bean Soup with Hardy Greens, 98
Italian, in Cranberry Beans Simmered with Sage, Sausages & Tomatoes, 64
Italian, in Polenta Pasticciata di Mama Elin, 132

**SEAWEED**
Kombu, in cooking beans, 27
Nori, in Sort-of Furikake, 231

**SESAME SEEDS,** see also Tahini
Dukkah, 230
Elkdream Bars, 222
Fruit and Nut Energy Bars, 224
Overnight Oatmeal-Sesame Pancakes, 128
Sort-of Furikake, 231
Winter Squash Stew with Purple Barley, 172

**SCARLET RUNNER BEANS**
Bean Salad with Wheat Berries and Quinoa, 90

**SLAW**
Crunchy Cabbage, Carrot & Radish Slaw, 59

**SOUP AND STEW**
Barley Beef Stew with Mushrooms, 162
Bulgur Wheat Soup with Lentils and Winter Greens, 164
Curried Lentil Soup, 95
Frikeh and Buttermilk Soup, 166
Indian Woman Yellow Bean Soup with Hardy Greens, 98
Joanna's Chili, 66
Late Summer Lentil Stew with Roasted Vegetables, 96
Lemony Garbanzo Bean Soup, 104
Minestrone with Wheat Berries and Arugula Pesto, 168
North African-Style Garbanzo Bean Stew, 100
Ribollita, 102

Smoky Tomato Soup with Quinoa, 170
Winter Squash Stew with Purple
   Barley, 172

**SPELT, FLOUR**
Dried Fruit and Nut Crostini, 212
Hazelnut Crackers, 214
Spelt-Hazelnut Cookies, 185
Spicy Nutty Apple Rye Muffins, 178

**SPICES**
Dukkah, 230
Tarka, Nabiha's Father's, 53
Tarka, Simple, 51
*Toasting and grinding, 35*

**SPINACH**
Bean Burgers with Greens 'n Grains, 84
Mediterranean-Style Pasta and Beans, 68
Roast Roots 'n Rye, 156
Roasted Garbanzos with Garlic and
   Greens, 62

**SQUASH, WINTER**
Black Bean, Chorizo & Rice Stew, 70
Indian Woman Yellow Bean Soup
   with Hardy Greens, 98
North African-Style Garbanzo Bean
   Stew, 100
Roast Roots 'n Rye, 156
Winter Squash Stew with Purple
   Barley, 172

**SUNFLOWER SEEDS**
Cilantro and Toasted Pumpkin Seed
   Sauce, 72
Elkdream Bars, 222

**SWEDISH BROWN BEANS**
Farmor's Bruna Bönar, 78

**SWISS CHARD,** see Chard

**TAHINI**
Homemade Falafel, 82
Lemon-Garlic Tahini Sauce, 83

**TEFF, FLOUR**
Teff and Ricotta Pancakes with
   Apple Topping, 126

Teff Chocolate Chip Cookies,
   Two Ways, 186

**TEFF, GRAIN**
Savory Teffolenta, 134
Teff and Ricotta Pancakes with Apple
   Topping, 126
Teff, Flax & Oatmeal Porridge, 123
Winter Teffolenta, 135

**TOMATILLOS**
Arikara Beans with Tomatillo Pork, 57
Quick Tomatillo Salsa, 87

**TOMATOES**
Basic Salsa, 199
Cannellini Beans with Grilled Tuna, 60
Chocolate Baked Rio Zape Beans, 76
Cranberry Beans Simmered with Sage,
   Sausages & Tomatoes, 64
Hominy with Chile and Tomato
   Braised Meat, 196
Indian Woman Yellow Bean Soup
   with Hardy Greens, 98
Joanna's Chili, 66
Late Summer Lentil Stew with
   Roasted Vegetables, 96
Lemony Garbanzo Bean Soup, 104
Mediterranean-Style Pasta and
   Beans, 68
Minestrone with Wheat Berries and
   Arugula Pesto, 168
Nabiha's Father's Way with Lentils, 52
Polenta Pasticciata di Mama Elin, 132
Ribollita, 102
Romesco Sauce, 228
Savory Teffolenta, 134
Slow-Roasted Tomatoes, 54
Smoky Tomato Soup with Quinoa, 170
Spanish Sofrito Sauce, 55
Summer Grain Salad, 160
Tortillas, 198
Wheat Berries Arrabiata with
   Poached Eggs, 142

**TUNA**
Cannellini Beans with Grilled Tuna, 60

**TURNIPS**
Minestrone with Wheat Berries and Arugula Pesto, 168
Winter White Bean Dip with Turnips, Lemon & Sage, 42

**WALNUTS**
Barley Mushroom Terrine, 136
Cranberry Beans & Rye Patties with Sage & Walnuts, 80
Dried Fruit and Nut Crostini, 212
Elin's Basil Pesto, 227
*Harvesting*, 209
Lemon-Walnut Cilantro Sauce, 44
Not Your Nonna's Biscotti, 188
Teff Chocolate Chip Cookies, Version II, 187
Walnut-Olive Spread, 225

**WHEAT, BERRIES**
Bean Salad with Wheat Berries and Quinoa, 90
Crockpot Grain Party Porridge, 121
Dolce di Grano, 184
Minestrone with Wheat Berries and Arugula Pesto, 168
Summer Grain Salad, 160
Wheat Berries Arrabiata with Poached Eggs, 142
Wheat Berry Pilaf, 151
Wheat Berry Salad with Broccoli, Apple, Hazelnuts & Smoked Salmon, 158

**WHEAT, FLOUR**
A Simple Fruit Crumble, 183
Basic Whole Grain Pancakes, 124
Chef Zachary's Unbelievable Buttermilk Biscuits, 182
Chia Seed and Buckwheat Pancakes, 125
Claudia's Hazelnut Cookies, 217
Dried Fruit and Nut Crostini, 212
Farmor's Limpa, 202
Not Your Nonna's Biscotti, 188
Overnight Oatmeal-Sesame Pancakes, 128
Spicy Nutty Apple Rye Muffins, 178

**WHITE BEANS**
Bean Burgers with Greens 'n Grains, 84
Eunice's Yellow-Eyed Baked Beans, 74
Mediterranean-Style Pasta and Beans, 68
Winter White Bean Dip with Turnips, Lemon & Sage, 42

**WHITE EMERGO BEANS**
Ribollita, 102

**WINTER SQUASH,** see Squash, Winter

**YELLOW-EYE BEANS**
Eunice's Yellow-Eyed Baked Beans, 74
Winter Squash Stew with Purple Barley, 172

**YIN-YANG BEANS,** see Calypso Beans

**YOGHURT**
Cilantro and Toasted Pumpkin Seed Sauce, 72
Lemon-Dill Yoghurt Sauce, 146
Lemon-Garlic Tahini Sauce, 83
Raita for Curried Lentil Soup, 94
Tzatziki, 83

**ZUCCHINI**
Savory Teffolenta, 134
Mediterranean-Style Pasta and Beans, 68
Minestrone with Wheat Berries and Arugula Pesto, 168

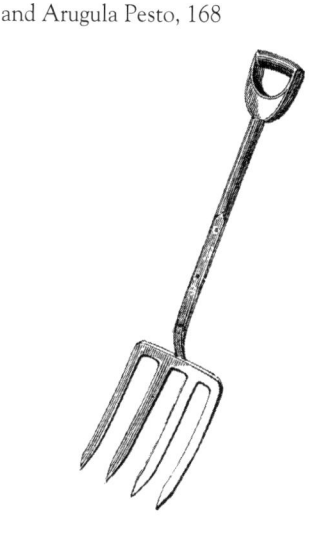

# IDEAS, NOTES & RECIPES

# IDEAS, NOTES & RECIPES